MISUSE OF POWER

How the Far Right Gained and Misuses Power

Ed Asner and Burt Hall

"This is not a battle between Republicans and Democrats...it is between the ultra right-wing element, who want to mold us in their image only, and those of us who want to preserve an open, free nation with real possibilities for the future for our children and grandchildren."

—A moderate Republican

D08898884

Mayhaven Publishing
P O Box 557
Mahomet, IL 61853
USA

Cover Design by Aaron Porter
Copyright © 2005 Ed Asner and Burt Hall
First Edition—First Printing 2005
1 2 3 4 5 6 7 8 9 10
Library of Congress Control Number: 2005928694
ISBN 1-932278-14-1 ISBN 13 978-1932278-14-9
Printed in Canada

Note: We have made every effort to provide clear and informative references to
the text. We have also listed a number of other sources in the event the reader
would like to seek further information. Please bring any error to our attention.

We dedicate this book to the 9/11 families.
We also dedicate this to our chief editor, Lynn Hall.

Preface

This small volume tells the story of the demise of American democracy over the past decade and a half. The purpose of the book is to provide in one readily accessible place what the American people need to know to take back their democracy. Of course, critics of American political life will point out that we never had the full democracy promised to us in the Declaration of Independence and the preamble to the U.S. Constitution. We were making progress, with many ups and downs, until the onslaught of vicious far-right politics hit us during Bill Clinton's presidency. This book is a call to action for those Americans who care enough about realizing the promise of our democracy to fight back.

Ed Asner

Notes From Ed Asner

My first brush with politics occurred when I became a labor rights activist during the 1980 strike by the Screen Actor's Guild, which delayed the 1980-81 TV season. As a result of working on behalf of fellow actors it was thought I had become a viable candidate for the Guild's presidency, and I went on to win the election in 1981. After Ronald Reagan's election, I became increasingly vocal against U.S. public policy, in particular affecting U.S. involvement in Latin America. Although the *Lou Grant* show was steadily gaining an audience and I was finding roles in feature films such as *Fort Apache*, *The Bronx* with Paul Newman, I was so naïve politically that I could never have guessed my political involvements would impact my career in such a negative manner.

I had first joined on to the El Salvador cause when a Catholic nun showed me pictures a Belgian photographer had taken of the atrocities being done by the death squads. I said: "Our country is giving them all kinds of military help? This is what's going on down there with government approval?" So I began to speak out.

When I took part in a fundraiser to send medical aid to El Salvador, conservative Screen Actor's Guild members, including Charlton Heston, raked me over the coals. I was seen as chief spokesman for Medical Aid for El Salvador, and the Reaganites loudly accused me of being a collaborator with the leftist guerrillas the United States was trying to crush.

When I took up the cause of El Salvador, I never thought it was going to be so controversial, but I paid for it. And so did those close to me. Apparently, the *Mary Tyler Moore Show's* co-creator and writer Allan Burns' assessment of the subsequent harassment went like this: "I've never seen anybody transformed so quickly from being everyone's favorite uncle to a communist swine."

Kimberly-Clark had two factories in El Salvador. They withdrew their sponsorship of the *Lou Grant* show along with other sponsors. There were two different congressional proposals for blacklisting the show and, of course, Charlton Heston was conducting his campaign against me at the same time. Eventually *Lou Grant* was canceled. CBS stated the cancellation was based on dwindling ratings, but I have always felt it was the dues I was forced to pay for my political involvements.

I certainly didn't think that I was waving any red flag. I thought I was calling attention to a humane problem. But as I said, work dried up, and there were personal threats—even bomb threats.

I was hired to narrate a national documentary in the Boston area, and just prior to that, I had done a radio interview out of Washington in which I mentioned my blacklisting. The first day I showed up for this documentary the producer took me to lunch and he said, "Remember that interview in Washington you gave?" I said, "Yeah." He said, "Well, that caught my attention. That's why you're here." I said, "What do you mean?" He replied, "Oh, about six months to a year ago, I had another documentary, and I put your name on the list for narrator and your name came back with a red line crossed through it. I knew what they meant, and I didn't do anything about it."

Not until 1985 did I land another television role.

The First Amendment is most precious, and yet it's meaningless to people when they don't have the guts to practice it. Our forefathers went to the trouble of creating this amendment so people could speak out, but few use it. Look at our 'leaders' in Washington. The policy seems to be, "keep your mouth shut, get along, go along." *The Los Angeles Times* used to have a labor reporter, and back then you could read about labor, limitedly, as opposed to the whole section devoted to stocks, bonds, and capital. Now there is a freeze-out. You cannot find equitable coverage in any paper, either on labor or across the board on politics, especially the Iraq 'invasion.' I don't call it a 'war,'—after all, Iraq's army was disbanded, sent home as we launched the invasion.

How do porcupines make love? Very carefully. How do Americans take stands against the far-right agenda? Very carefully. When I took a stand on our continuing to arm the murderous junta that ruled El Salvador, or the Contras who were busy assassinating in Nicaragua, it was based on humanitarian grounds. In those days I was dismissed as a Communist. Today there is no Communist threat and yet, should a citizen raise doubts about governmental policy, they are still discredited as if the Russian bear was still pulling the strings. Congress, the media, educators, judges, and all other potential whistleblowers have no platform from which to be heard due to the far-right's discrediting of opposing views. Evolution, pro-choice, labor organizing, toxic air and water, land and species preservation, deficits, homelessness, illiteracy, prisons bursting at the seams— where are the spokespersons?

I hope you will use your very precious freedom to speak out forcibly on issues that are important to you. But, first, you need to better understand the politics of the far right. I hope this book will help, for it gives a concise lead up to this Administration's engagement and pursuit of a war that should never have been fought, and of an administration that governs with methods and policies that Americans were never taught to believe in.

Notes From Burt Hall

I was formerly a Group Director (analyst) on matters of national security with the U.S. Government Accountability office. During my tenure with GAO, I also worked several years on loan to a congressional commission and the Office of Management and Budget. I served in World War II, am a graduate of the Harvard Advanced Management Program, and co-authored, with my wife, Lynn Hall, the best-selling book, *How the Experts Win at Bridge*. I have authored a number of articles, including three with Ed Asner on terrorism strategy, 9/11 responsibility, and the war in Iraq.

Over the years I have voted for both Democratic and Republican presidents. In 2000, I became a registered Republican to support Senator John McCain's bid for the presidency. I am progressive on some issues and conservative on others, and I am guided by logic, common sense, and American values.

My first encounter with the far right occurred during the House Impeachment of President Bill Clinton. My wife and I had recently joined *MoveOn*, whose goal was convincing Congress to censure the

President and move on with the country's business.

Forty members of *MoveOn*, from all over the country, went to Washington at our own expense to deliver several hundred thousand petitions to Congress. They were signed by Democrats, Republicans, and Independents.

First, we submitted all the petitions to House Speaker Bob Livingston's office, where I also left a personal letter. Next, we delivered constituent petitions to every congressman's office. I delivered the petitions to about 15 offices. Practically all of them were accepted graciously. The one notable exception was the office of Tom DeLay, the House Whip at that time. Later I discovered that his office was using unethical practices at that very moment to force impeachment through the House.

I feel confident that our petitions, plus other public outcry, did some good. At the last minute, the House Speaker did try to switch the House to censure and stop the unlawful impeachment—but he failed. As discussed in this book, some House members immediately regretted their vote and two of the most important principals now regret they participated.

Since that experience I've followed with interest, and great concern, the actions of the far right and their efforts to take total control of our government. I hope this book will enlighten you about what is really going on, because we all need to work together to rescue this country from its current downward spiral.

It has been a pleasure to co-author this book with Ed Asner.

Lynn and Burt Hall

Table of Contents

Chapter Six

Far Right Continues To Misuse Power In Second Term   149

Appendix I   183

Appendix II   187

Acknowledgements   192

Chapter One

OVERVIEW

"We are an 'endangered species'…my wing of the
party has been swept into oblivion by the ultra
right, which now controls the Republican agenda."

—*A moderate Republican*

This book describes how the current far-right administration came to power and has improperly governed our country. Each of the chapters that follow expand on and document this overview.

The far right has hijacked the Republican Party and poses the greatest danger to our nation's welfare in decades. Desperate to further their own agenda, they abuse power and do not play by the rules or follow the U.S. Constitution. They decide what they want to do without regard to ethics, legality, or long-term consequences, then pursue a win-at-any-cost strategy to achieve their goals.

Influence of the far right can be found in all parts of our society—the religious right, business, the legal community, the political establishment, media, foundations, educational institutions, and think tanks. They include the relatively-new Republican extremists, often referred to as neo-cons. They use aggressive propaganda to achieve radical change and justify mistakes. To make things happen, the far right is willing to distort, conceal, misrepresent—and trample those who stand in their way.

The far right's quest for power gained momentum in the 1990's when they first took control of the House of Representatives. Soon they declared war on the Clinton administration. Initially, they engineered a series of worthless investigations designed to wreck his Administration, wasting well over 100 million taxpayer dollars. Even though they came up empty-handed, they refused to clear the President of these investigations until his two terms ended.

Frustrated because they had failed to incriminate the President, the far right stumbled on a chance to manipulate our judicial system and ambush him for a personal indiscretion. Then, they misled and intimidated the Attorney General to get control of the investigation. To complete their duplicity, the far right blocked all efforts to censure the President and railroaded his impeachment in a lame-duck session. They used political blackmail to get the necessary congressional votes. (Chp. 2)

The resulting impeachment was unconstitutional and defied the intent of our founding fathers. The far right knew the Senate would not convict; their real purpose was to force the President to resign. That plan didn't work, but the resulting media frenzy laid the groundwork for a far-right takeover of the White House in 2001.

While Congress and the nation were distracted by the far right's assault on the presidency, al-Qaeda declared war and attacked the United States several times. With tunnel vision, House leaders continued with their illegitimate impeachment. As the 9/11 Commission has pointed out, Congress bears some responsibility for the 9/11 disaster, because for several years it failed to confront global terrorism and call for necessary changes in government.

With the emergence of the Bush administration in 2001, the far right now controlled all three branches of government. Under their leadership, our country has piled up a crushing debt for future generations, and has suffered reversals in both domestic and foreign policy. The most prominent foreign policy reversal was the mishandling of the war on terror, both *before and after* 9/11.

In its zeal to further the far right's agenda, the new Administration left the nation totally unprepared for one of the worst disasters in U.S. history. When they took office in early 2001, President Bush and his key advisors were given strong advice and urgent warnings about the al-Qaeda threat from top-level experts, representing both the current and previous administrations, and including the former president. That spring and summer the Administration continued to receive advice on the gravity of the threat, and repeated and unprecedented warnings from around the world. These warnings included possible use of hijacked commercial aircraft as weapons. (Chp. 3)

The Bush administration basically put the al-Qaeda threat on a back burner and didn't even try to defend against the oncoming attack. The attitude and inaction of the President and his far-right advisors contributed to 9/11. Their negligence exposed our nation to untold financial damage and, more importantly, to great loss of precious human life.

The President has evaded any responsibility for the disaster and even attempted to block a review of what happened. When that didn't work, he stonewalled the 9/11 Investigative Commission for more than a year. Because of the approaching presidential election, the 9/11 Commission strongly believed that any attempt to assess responsibility at the highest level of government would create disunity within their own ranks, and the resulting partisan fight would jeopardize the Commission's report. (Chp. 3)

After faltering *before* 9/11, the President responded aggressively to the 9/11 attack, but his response was short-lived. Within months, he and his far-right advisors embarked on a one-year path to war in Iraq, a country that had nothing to do with 9/11 and represented no threat to the United States. During this time the President and Vice President misused their office by:

- Urging the nation on to war, while giving the CIA very little time to estimate the threat for congressional review.

- Presenting threat information to Congress and the American people as absolute fact, when such assessments are inherently uncertain.

- Dismissing findings of international inspectors who were on the ground in Iraq. These findings discounted our intelligence and could have prevented war.

Subsequent congressional and presidential investigations into pre-war intelligence were blocked from looking at: (1) whether the President's *desire* to go to war unduly influenced the intelligence, (2) how Administration top officials used that intelligence, and (3) how the intelligence was presented to

Congress and the American people. This lack of accountability can be anticipated whenever an extreme element of one political party controls both the executive and congressional branches of government.

President Bush has tried to justify his actions by saying he was spreading democracy in the Mideast. Over the past century many American presidents have promoted democracy around the world with excellent results. President Bush's use of the policy, however, has devastated the country of Iraq, caused great loss of life, and wasted several hundred billion dollars. There were better options than going to war, and the President chose the wrong way to spread freedom. (Chp. 4)

Meanwhile, al-Qaeda is still a major threat to the U.S. The scope of the President's policy for the war on terror has been too limited to deal with a global problem. The policy does not address the root causes of terrorism—the *only* way to reduce the continuing threat to the United States. A more appropriate and comprehensive policy would identify and seek to reverse root causes, and would engage all heads of state in a program to dismantle terrorist activities. Chapter 4 outlines such a broad policy, as well as two options to exit Iraq with honor.

In the build-up to war, neither Congress nor the media challenged misjudgments of the Bush far-right administration. Both of these vital institutions failed the American people. (Chp. 4)

Much of the media has relinquished its independence and acceded to government power and increasing control of big business. Congress should hold public hearings on the massive concentration of media ownership and the conflict of interest that exists between ownership and the people's right to be informed in a fair and impartial manner.

Chapter 5 is a satire on the war in Iraq. It will provide the reader with some insight into what *might* have happened in the inner sanctums of the White House, as Bush and his far-right advisors shifted their focus away from our major terrorism threat and, instead, hunkered down to plot a war in Iraq.

The final chapter highlights the beginning of the President's second term and points out examples of how the far right continues to misuse power. It shows that our country is still headed in the wrong direction and toward a fiscal train wreck.

The radical agenda of the far right has moved the Republican Party away from the American mainstream. The final chapter suggests a number of major changes in direction. To accomplish this, we need new leadership—a strong moderate from either political party—to get our country back on track. To assist this new leader, all of us must carefully reassess our representation in Congress.

The Bottom Line

The far right now enjoys the balance of power and will do whatever it takes to keep it. According to a recent article in the *Washington Post*, the far right is solidifying their gains by reshaping Congress and the courts in their image and by centralizing control of government. As a result, we are being moved toward a one-party rule. As you read through the various chapters supporting this overview, consider the impact a powerful Executive Branch and one-party rule will have on our democracy. Will there be any checks and balances or accountability? Will the minority in Congress have a real opportunity to participate? Will there be Congressional oversight and public scrutiny? Will there be increased government secrecy and control over information? Will policy decisions be limited to a small group reporting to the president and leaders of Congress?

Chapter Two

Far Right Subverts Presidency To Regain White House

As indicated in the overview, the far right decides what they want to do and then pursues a win-at-any-cost strategy to achieve their goals. They assume they have a "divine" right to tear down those who do not share their beliefs.

In the 1990's the far right refused to accept the results of national elections and declared war on the Clinton administration. They tried every means at their disposal—unethical and illegal—to undermine the Administration and force the President to resign.

To destabilize the presidency they launched a series of investigations that turned up nothing. They refused to clear him, however, until he left office. In a last-ditch effort to wreck his Administration, the far right:

- Manipulated our judicial system to set a perjury trap for the President's personal indiscretion.

- Used incomplete and false information and intimidated the Attorney General to get control of the investigation.

- Advocated impeachment in violation of the Independent Counsel statute.

- Railroaded the President's impeachment in defiance of the U.S. Constitution and views of most Americans.

- Used political blackmail to get the necessary congressional votes.

These acts distracted and disrupted our government, the media, and the nation. They precluded any well-considered response to several terrorist attacks, and left the nation vulnerable to additional ones. Subversive politics not only undermined the Clinton administration, but eased the way for the far right to take control of the White House in 2001. It all started with the:

Refusal to Accept 1992 Presidential Election Results

After much campaigning and political infighting, we elect a president every four years. Then, traditionally, the country pulls together and supports the elected president. Threats to our country unify us even more. That tradition was broken in the 1990's.

Previously, the opposition party had owned the White House for 12 years and was outraged at the loss of the presidency. Clinton was seen as a usurper, his victory had to be illegitimate and he had to be driven from the White House. To accomplish this, he had to be brought down.

As a result, in the aftermath of Clinton's election, far-right members of the business and legal communities, church organizations, and the political establishment collectively mounted covert and other efforts to disable the President's administration and remove him from office. Their tentacles spread far and wide. A few of the players were:

- Investment bankers Peter Smith and Richard Mellon Scaife, both of whom paid huge sums to finance any possible scandal—no matter how far fetched. Scaife is believed to have spent from $200 to $300 million trying to influence government policy and "steer this country to his brand of hard-core conservatism." He financed a right-wing magazine, *American Spectator,* whose role was to trash the President, without much regard for the facts, and drive him from office.[1]

- Richard Porter, Kenneth Starr's law partner and member of the first Bush administration, and Theodore Olson, a member of both Bush administrations. They were actively involved behind the scenes, playing important roles in various assaults on the President. Olson participated in several Scaife-funded activities and was intent on undermining the Clinton presidency without disclosing his own involvement.[2]

- Jerry Falwell and Pat Robertson who represented the opposition from the religious right. Falwell's organization, for example, promoted videotapes accusing the President of drug-dealing and the murder of White House aid, Vince Foster—among other things.[3]

- A group from Arkansas who stood ready and willing to feed the far-right network. They included political opponents incensed over Clinton's success, and financial opportunists. The "Arkansas Project," sponsored by Scaife, was a four-year, $2.4 million attempt to gather information "leading to political ruin of the President."[4]

- Newt Gingrich, who became the new right-wing Speaker of the House in 1994. Gingrich called the Clinton administration "the enemy of normal Americans" and said in a private meeting he would use "subpoena power" to wage war against the White House. He envisioned as many as 20 congressional investigations being conducted simultaneously.[5] Smith and Scaife were both major contributors to Gingrich's campaigns and causes.[6] Soon Gingrich would try to use a government shut-down to force an unacceptable budget on the President—a violation of the U.S. Constitution.

- Tom DeLay, then the House Majority Whip. Following a third terrorist attack on the United States, he diverted the nation and Congress from confronting this menace by using extraordinary measures to force an illegitimate impeachment of the President.[7]

These facts, and those which follow, are just a small part of far-right activities documented by highly reputable journalists and five recently-published books: *The Hunting of the President*, *A Vast Conspiracy*, *Blinded by the Right*, *The Breach: Inside the Impeachment and Trial of William Jefferson Clinton* and *The Clinton Wars*.

Plot to Manipulate Our Judicial System

The Paula Jones incident first surfaced in an *American Spectator* article by David Brock. He later expressed regret for having written it and confessed to using innuendo and unverified charges to spice up his material. He received $5000 from Peter Smith to begin researching the article. Brock found out later that Smith had paid another $30,000 to his sources of the article (known in the trade as "cash for trash").[8]

Richard Porter (Starr's partner) formed a group of lawyers to support and advise Paula Jones.[9] Rather than sue *American Spectator* magazine, her advisors decided to advance their own agenda by working covertly to manipulate the courts in a sexual harassment suit against the President. Referred to as the "elves," they kept their participation a secret from their own law firms.[10]

Before taking over the job of Independent Counsel, Starr himself offered to work free for Jones. He also had six telephone conversations with Jones' lawyers, in which he offered *his* opinion that presidents were not immune from civil suits. He stated publicly several times that the suit should proceed without delay.[10a]

Scaife donated $50,000 to help Jones sue the President. A member of Gingrich's House staff would be her chief fundraiser. People close to the case suspected that anything that happened between the two principals was consensual, but they pursued it to humiliate the President and hasten his destruction.

The plan was to set a perjury trap when the case came to court by interrogating the President about past relationships. This plot was pursued well before and independent of the Lewinsky matter.[11]

Independent Counsel Secretly Replaced with Kenneth Starr

Following Republican demands for inquiry into a failed Arkansas Whitewater land deal, which took place in the 1980's, Attorney General Reno appointed special counsel Robert Fiske to investigate Whitewater, as well as the President and First Lady's involvement.[12] In the next several months Fiske moved fast, initiating several local prosecutions in Arkansas. Unexpectedly, a three-judge panel replaced him with Starr. They did so after ultra-right Senators, Jesse Helms and Lauch Faircloth, secretly put pressure on the panel.[13]

The switching of a sitting independent counsel was improper because Fiske was aggressively pursuing the Whitewater case and had impeccable credentials and a reputation for fairness. In addition, Starr had no investigative experience and opposed Clinton on every major issue of the day. Starr was the "designated point man in a strategy...to destabilize the Clinton presidency."[14]

Despite his few qualifications, additional investigations were added to Starr's plate. They included White House travel office firings, possible misuse of FBI files, and Vince Foster's suicide.[15] Starr now had four investigations of the President. Then, Starr went beyond his authorized scope to make numerous inquiries into Clinton's private sex life while Governor of Arkansas. This was a fifth—unauthorized—investigation.[16]

Eventually, Starr would spend $70 million trying to bring down the Clinton presidency. Other Independent Counsels spent another $40 million investigating members of his Administration. In the end, not one top official was convicted of a public crime.[17]

Starr Resigns Temporarily

Recognizing that any case against the Clintons was over, Starr's best people began leaving his employ. Those who stayed on were "the unemployable and the obsessed."[18] Suddenly, Starr announced plans to accept a teaching position at Pepperdine University in California—without closing *any* of his investigations. The new position had been arranged earlier by Scaife.

The far right and the media were stunned. The Washington press corps had succumbed to allegations of Clinton's wrongdoing, but Starr couldn't prove them. Outraged, William Safire of the *New York Times* described Starr as "a man with a warped sense of duty" who "had brought shame on the legal profession by walking out on his client—the people of the United States."[19]

Meanwhile, the far right had published a futuristic book, *The Impeachment of William Jefferson Clinton*. It *imagined* Clinton's payment of hush money during the Whitewater investigation and his later impeachment. The book had an anonymous author—widely rumored to be Ted Olson—and included a forward from a congressional right-winger, Republican Bob Barr, saying it was, "....required reading for every citizen of this country."[20]

The far right continued to hope Starr would inflict a mortal wound on the President. This was a theme of Ted Olson's anonymous satire in *American Spectator*. Bombarded by protests and attacks on his reputation, Starr decided to stay on.[21]

High Court Blunders

Meanwhile, the Supreme Court allowed the Jones sexual harassment suit to go forward during the President's term in office on the grounds that it would *not* be a distraction. The Dean of American Journalism, David Broder, explained the Court's decision this way:

> "One of the great blunders of American history
> ...one of the dumbest decisions in the long history
> of the Court....when they decided that a President
> should have no immunity against civil suits while
> serving in office, they may have broken their own
> record for ignoring reality." [22]

Under our Constitution, once a president assumes office he owes the public his full time and attention. Civil suits can tie-up a president's hands during his term in office, especially controversial ones. During an *NBC* interview, Jones acknowledged the disruption her suit could create and said she was willing to wait until the President's term was over. However, the Supreme Court placed her case above the public good—a clear departure from the U.S. Constitution.

Years later, Jones would publicly admit, on the *Larry King Show*, to being used by people with a political agenda.

Empty Handed—Starr Forces His Way into Judicial Plot

These were desperate times for Starr and his men. They had drilled dry holes concerning the Clintons for several years and their supporters were unhappy. Starr's people had given up on charging the President with any wrongdoing, but they were in no rush to close the cases or advise the Washington press corps.[23]

Suddenly, a new cast of characters surfaced—Linda Tripp and Lucienne Goldberg—less pleasantly named in the book, *American Rhapsody*—plus a reporter from *Newsweek*, Michael Isikoff. Tripp had illegally wiretapped her friend, Monica Lewinsky, and knew of her relationship with the President—one that he might deny when interrogated in the Jones case.[24]

Starr had no authority to intervene, but he moved fast. He went to the Justice Department and begged for more authority on the grounds of a link between the Lewinsky matter and his Whitewater land investigation. The presumed link in the two cases was the President's friend, Vernon Jordan.[25]

According to Starr's people, Jordan had given job assistance to Lewinsky in exchange for false testimony she would give for the President in the Jones case. Starr's people then pressured Attorney General Reno into a snap, overnight decision, by telling her that soon *Newsweek* would be reporting a sensational sex story and cover-up—including any refusal by Reno to let the Independent Counsel investigate.[26] In making their case, Starr's office provided incomplete and false information and omitted three conflicts of interest.

Starr Misleads the Justice Department

Newsweek's top echelon actually had decided not to publish the sexual affair. It was Reno's overnight approval that eventually tipped the scales.[27]

Starr's people omitted the important fact that Vernon Jordan's job assistance to Lewinsky started well before she had any inkling of getting a Jones subpoena. Jordan's assistance was not even the President's idea; it was Linda Tripp's. There never was any overlap with the Whitewater land deal.[28]

Starr Fails to Reveal Conflict of Interest

Starr did not disclose his previous involvements in the Jones case. He had a number of consultations with her lawyers, had advocated her case in public, and had offered to work free for her.[29]

Starr's office said they'd had no contact with the Jones team. Actually, they had already invaded the Jones case and were in collusion with Jones' advisors—the "elves." These were the people assembled to covertly assist her without their firm's knowledge.[30]

Starr did not disclose that his law partner (Porter) was conspiring behind the scenes to undermine the presidency, as well as to further the Jones plot (see pp. 30 and 32).[31]

After getting the new authority, Starr's people implored *Newsweek* to hold up publication of the sex story until the President had answered the Jones deposition—the long-awaited ambush was set.[32]

Justice Accepts False Information—Ok's Starr Investigation

The Independent Counsel statute was clear. Attorney General Reno had to make a preliminary review herself and find "credible evidence" before the statute could be triggered. Had she done so, she would have found (1) the suspicions about Vernon Jordan were untrue, (2) there were no grounds for expanding Starr's authority and (3) several conflicts of interest undermined Starr's capacity to do an independent and impartial review.[33]

The problem with Reno's overnight decision is that the Independent Counsel statute did not operate on suspicions or hearsay, but on evidence determined to be credible by Justice Department officials. Further, Starr had an axe to grind and was not the right person for the job. Reno pulled the trigger too fast, too soon, and worst of all based on bad information.

Unfortunately, her ill-advised decision triggered a situation impossible to control—the assignment of a sex scandal to a biased team of investigators with an unlimited budget, who were intent on finally getting the President.

A few weeks after Starr got his 6th investigation, the presiding judge dismissed the Jones lawsuit and concluded that the Lewinsky matter was not material to that case. So, now we have Starr abandoning several unfinished investigations to chase obstruction in a sexual harassment case—and there was no genuine case to obstruct.

Starr Violates Statute to Advocate Impeachment

As Bob Woodward of the *Washington Post* reported, Starr's decision to send a massive narrative of the Clinton-Lewinsky sexual relationship to Congress was "pathetic and unwise."[34] To the dismay of many, House far-right leaders made the report immediately available to everyone—including children—in excruciating detail, via the Internet.

The history and charter of the Office of Independent Counsel is clear; he is a prosecutor and fact-giver, not an impeachment advocate for a particular political party in power. Because of his strong advocacy, Starr's ethics adviser, Sam Dash, immediately resigned. Dash said that by acting as the House's "prosecuting counsel for impeachment," Starr had violated the statute requiring him to present evidence but not conclusions.[35]

Impeachment Thought to be Dead on Arrival

Well over two-thirds of the American people favored Clinton remaining in office and made their views known by rendering a huge setback to Republicans during midterm elections. At this juncture, impeachment was for all practical purposes dead.[36]

In late summer 1998, just as *The Starr Report* was being released, our country suffered its third terrorist attack—the bombing of two U.S. embassies, killing over 200 people and injuring about 5000. At that time Bin Laden declared war on the United States, saying "to kill the Americans—civilians or military—is an individual duty for every Muslim."[37]

The two earlier terrorist attacks involved bombings of the World Trade Center in 1993, killing 6 and injuring others, and of American facilities in Saudi Arabia in 1996, killing 19 U.S. military personnel and wounding nearly 400.

In 2000, there would be a fourth attack—on the *U.S.S. Cole,* killing eleven and wounding others—and the fifth attack would be 9/11, killing 3000.

Ed Asner and Burt Hall

Impeachment Railroaded
Despite Terror Attacks/War Declaration

Two decades earlier, House impeachment proceedings led to President Nixon's resignation for abuses of power and misconduct in office. The House's action depended on three things: (1) factually-based hearings with witnesses, (2) bipartisan cooperation, and (3) statesmanship. All three of these were conspicuously missing in the impeachment of President Clinton.

Earlier, Chairman Hyde of the Judiciary committee had promised the American people a fair hearing on the Starr report. However, the Republican setback in midterm elections reduced their majority in the next Congress to almost nothing. Instead of a deliberative, bipartisan approach, far-right House leaders moved with all the speed of "The Roadrunner." The "lame-duck" House called no witnesses, conducted partisan hearings, and had only party-line votes.[38] *The President's lawyers had to testify without knowledge of what the charges would be.*[39]

Without waiting for cessation of U.S. military operations over Iraq for UN violations, far-right leaders drove two impeachment articles through a final House vote in December, just days before the people's newly-elected Congress would convene. At the last minute, Speaker Livingston reversed himself saying, "We've got to stop this...this is crazy." He called an emergency meeting of his leadership, stating, "We're going to have a censure vote." But others prevailed on him to continue.[40]

The House action was a rush to judgment never before witnessed on a matter of such profound importance. A few moderate Republicans refused to go along. Several others *immediately* regretted their vote and said so publicly—but it was too late.[41]

DeLay's Real Mission—Force the President to Resign

As documented in Peter Baker's *The Breach*, powerful Majority Whip, Tom DeLay, stepped into the leadership vacuum and persuaded incoming Speaker, Bob Livingston, to block a censure alternative. Censure was the one option favored by most Americans and many in Congress. Orchestrating events from behind the scenes, DeLay succeeded in crushing all attempts to consider censure the moment they arose. As a result, moderate congressmen on both sides had no middle ground to vote their consciences.

DeLay realized the Senate would not convict. His real mission was to drive Clinton from office—first impeach, and then force him to resign. He ordered his staff to "dedicate yourselves to it or leave" [his employ]..."to work day and night." He took this step in mid-August 1998, well *before* Starr submitted his report to Congress.[42]

On left, Tom DeLay with then House Speaker Bob Livingston

—photo by Karin Cooper, *Liaison Agency*

Throughout, DeLay took absolute control, and left nothing to chance. For example, he set up a special "evidence room" where he and his deputies would send undecided House members. This room included allegations which not even Starr saw fit to publish, much of it uncorroborated and undocumented.[43] Using his powerful Whip position, DeLay applied intense pressure on House members who were wavering or on the fence by:

- Threatening loss of their chairmanship.

- Threatening to arrange a strong challenge to them in their next congressional race.

- Threatening to turn fund raisers and party officials against them.

- Threatening to expose them to their constituents if they visited the "evidence room" and still cleared Clinton.[44]

A member of DeLay's office staff told one Republican congressman who opposed impeachment, "...the next two years would be the longest of his life." Later, Bob Woodward would report that Chairman Hyde was willing to entertain censure had his leadership been willing.[45]

Public Up in Arms—Petitions Congress

Much of the public was alarmed by what was going on in Congress, but were unable to stop it.

As just one example: a young couple in California set up an organization on the Internet called *Censure* and *MoveOn (www.moveon.org)*.[46] Eventually, about 40 *MoveOn* volunteers went to Washington, at their own expense, to deliver more than 300,000 anti-impeachment petitions to House members from their constituents. In addition, *MoveOn* delivered, in the presence of the media, a full set of the petitions to the House Speaker's office. These petitions urged the House to censure the President and move on with the country's business. They were signed by Democrats, Republicans, and Independents alike.[47]

MoveOn volunteers also made 250,000 phone calls and sent a million e-mails to Congress. Millions of other people expressed opposition—eventually; lines of communication to Washington broke down.[48]

Far Right Defies U.S. Constitution and Founding Fathers

Former President Ford said an impeachable offense "is whatever a majority of the House of Representatives considers it to be at a given moment in history." But the history of impeachment shows he must have been jesting.[49]

The House Judiciary committee said it would establish standards to guide their impeachment process. These standards were never set.

The impeachment of a president is a modern day, civilized alternative to assassination of a king. To avoid Britain's partisan misuse of impeachment and because our constitutional framers distrusted legislatures, they limited its use to *grave breaches* of official duties, specifically *treason and bribery*. When our framers added "*other high crimes and misdemeanors,*" the term "*other*" obviously meant something on a similar plane with treason and bribery. The term *"high misdemeanors"* actually refers to serious offenses against the state as in 18th century England, not minor or trivial offenses as we interpret misdemeanors today. As one framer said, we are talking about *"great and dangerous offenses."*[50]

Four hundred historians and 430 law professors warned the House against impeachment. The law professors said members of Congress would violate their constitutional responsibilities if they sought to remove the President for reasons that fell short of constitutional standards. Many scholars agreed with George Mason's statement that impeachment must be for a great crime or an attempt to subvert the Constitution. Another founding father, James Madison, opposed a low standard because it would create a weak presidency serving at the pleasure of

Congress. The framers of our Constitution obviously wanted the highest possible bar for removal of a president.[51]

Alexander Hamilton warned "the greatest danger [is] that the decision [to impeach] will be regulated more by the comparative strength of the parties, than by the real demonstrations of innocence or guilt."[52] As a House member confirmed, the strength of the parties did, in fact, regulate the outcome.

> "When radical Republicans hijacked the Constitution and misused impeachment for partisan purposes, I worked on the House Judiciary Committee in an effort to stop them. We lost all the votes along party lines....While we couldn't dissuade Republicans in the House of Representatives, the overwhelming voice of Americans helped the United States Senate to end this madness."[53]
>
> —Representative Zoe Lofgren

Common sense tells us that our founding fathers put impeachment in the Constitution to deal with serious breaches of official duties and great crimes against society. If impeachment, instead, concerned such things as covering up a personal mistake, some of our founding fathers themselves would have been vulnerable, and some fine national leaders of the past would have been lost. The impeachment remedy was intended to preserve constitutional government by removing from office an official who subverts the office, not someone who covers up a private matter.[54]

The general public had expressed its displeasure with what was going on in the House of Representatives by voting a major Republican setback and by voicing their overwhelming objections. The public knew this was a private offense, not a public one against the state. They also knew there had to be a higher standard for removing a twice-elected president. The people who elected and reelected Clinton saw him as "a flawed but highly capable and essentially decent man." No evidence has ever emerged to connect Clinton's personal life with his performance as President.[55]

The same far-right religious leaders, who had worked to undermine Clinton's presidency, got nationwide media coverage by saying that America "*deserved*" the 9/11 disaster because of our cultural problems. Did the far right similarly make a personal, rather than constitutional, judgment that Clinton "*deserved*" impeachment, too? Like terrorists, does the extreme right believe they have a divine right to destroy those who do not share their beliefs? Was that really at the heart of Clinton's impeachment and efforts to wreck his Administration?

The Bottom Line

The misuse of our judicial system to plot a presidential downfall was unacceptable. Further, the Paula Jones case should have been stopped by the Supreme Court on constitutional grounds. A disruptive civil suit should never have been allowed to interfere with the President's official duties and his responsibilities to the American people.

Kenneth Starr had no authority to invade the President's private life. Even though misled by Starr, the Attorney General was in a position to stop his intrusion had she followed her own statutory review requirements and judicial ethics on conflicts of interest. Both Starr and Chairman Hyde have publicly confessed regret. In December 2004, Starr acknowledged that Whitewater and Lewinsky were "separate" matters and that he should *not* have led the Lewinsky one. Asked whether he would do the impeachment again, Chairman Hyde said, "I'm not sure. I might not."[56]

After Starr became a puppet of far-right House leaders and violated his own statute to advocate impeachment, DeLay's abuse of power forced it through the House. The impeachment had nothing to do with presidential performance and defied our Constitution and the intent of our founding fathers.

Rather than wasting time with impeachment, Congress should have focused on the nation's preparedness for global terrorism, especially since several attacks on the United States had already occurred.

The most precious thing we have in our democracy is the right to choose our local and national leaders, including the President of the United States. Subversive politics disrupted the nation and weakened both our presidency and national security. To prevent recurrence, Congress and the general public should consider these actions:

- Should a higher bar and time limit be set on congressionally-initiated investigations of a president? How can we condone clouding the presidency with a series of politically-motivated investigations and then allowing them to remain open throughout the president's term in office...without clearing him?

- What should be done about people who manipulate and misuse our judicial process to gain political advantage, at the expense of our national welfare?

- What should be done to prevent the use of impeachment as a tool to drive a president from office? Do we need congressional standards such as those intended by our founders?

While Clinton's personal behavior did leave a stain on his presidency, far-right leaders left an even larger stain on the House of Representatives. They disrupted the nation and diverted Congress from executing its own responsibilities. As the 9/11 Commission reported, "Congress took too little action to address the emerging terrorist threat." It "...gave little guidance to agencies, did not reform them to meet the threat, and did not perform robust oversight."

Achieving Congressional Accountability

Misuse of power subverted a duly-elected presidency and diverted the nation from the menace of global terrorism. The only sure way to prevent such abuses in the future is to have an informed public and hold those responsible personally accountable. Unless the radical right is held accountable for trying to nullify two presidential elections, our system of government will continue to be subjected to win-at-any-cost methods and could suffer even greater consequences.

As private citizens, we don't have to accept what happened. We can change things for the future. We can hold members of Congress accountable and improve the quality of leadership in that body. New campaign finance laws and the Internet give the average citizen much more influence in selecting their representatives. We need to support any viable candidate who will improve the quality of our national leadership. Through the powerful medium of the Internet, it is easier for millions of Americans to contribute small amounts of money and time to candidates of their choice.

Three House leaders responsible for abuses of power and constitutional violations are no longer in Congress. They have been removed (Gingrich), resigned (Livingston), and retired (Armey). A fourth (DeLay) is now Majority Leader, and a fifth (Hyde) still holds a chairmanship.

In recent times the House Ethics committee has admonished DeLay for attempted bribery to get a House member's vote and soliciting contributions for legislative favors. Several of his associates have been indicted for laundering illegal contributions and he is still under criminal investigation. DeLay has been involved in violations of House voting rules and an unfair redrawing of House districts to favor Republicans. He also misused Homeland Security resources to settle a dispute over the new districts. House Minority Leader Nancy Pelosi has declared DeLay "ethically unfit."[57]

In 2005, House Republican leadership replaced the Ethics Committee's Chairman and two other Republican members with representatives who were loyal to the far right. They also changed the Ethics Committee's rules to permit this new Republican membership to block any further investigation of DeLay. Following much opposition, these rule changes were overturned, but the new committee membership remains intact.

Both Hyde and DeLay are unfit for congressional leadership positions. Public pressure should be brought to strip Delay of his leadership role and Hyde of his chairmanship.

"How dare you bring a case so weak, so slight, so personal, so dirty, so intrusive, so rotten, so ugly, so without constitutional merit and so removed from any question of abuse of power? How dare you tie up Congress, the nation, the presidency and the government in a matter that involved only a man's personal life? How dare you invade my home, my marriage—expose matters that should be between husband and wife—who are you people, and what gave you the right to do this to us?"[58]

—Richard Cohen, *Washington Post,* describing imaginary
script for Hillary Clinton to speak in Well of Senate during
impeachment trial

Endnotes

1   Brock, David, *Blinded By the Right: The Conscience of an Ex-Conservative*, Crown Publishers, 2002, pp. 79-81.

2   Conason, Joe and Lyons, Gene, *The Hunting Of The President: The Ten-Year Campaign to Destroy Bill and Hillary Clinton*, St. Martin's Press, 2000, pp. 104-107, 259.

3   *Ibid*, pp. 139-153.

4   Ibid, p. 111.

5   Ibid, p. 174.

6   Toobin, Jeffrey, *A Vast Conspiracy*, Touchstone, 2000, pp. 81-82.

7   Blumenthal, Sidney, *The Clinton Wars*, Farrar, Strauss and Giroux, 2003, pp. 537-538.

8   Brock, *Blinded By the Right*, p. 143.

9   "Anti-Clinton Lawyers Kept Jones' Case Alive" Don Van Natta Jr. and Jill Abramson, *New York Times*, January 24, 1999.

10 Brock, *Blinded By the Right*, pp. 179-183.

10a "Anti-Clinton Lawyers Kept Jones' Case Alive" Don Van Natta Jr. and Jill Abramson, *New York Times*, January 24, 1999.

11 Brock, *Blinded By the Right*, pp. 184-185.

12 *Ibid*, pp. 190-191.

13 "Rulebook? What Rulebook?" Alan Ehrenhalt, *New York Times*.

14 Brock, *Blinded By the Right*, p. 188.

15 Toobin, *A Vast Conspiracy*, p. 93.

16 Brock, *Blinded By the Right*, p. 310.

17 Blumenthal, *The Clinton Wars*, p.791.

18 Toobin, *A Vast Conspiracy*, pp. 188-189.

19 *Ibid*, p. 94.

20 Brock, *Blinded By the Right*, p. 301.

21 Conason and Lyons, *The Hunting Of The President*, p. 259.

22 "With its cloudy decisions, Supreme Court ignores reality" David Broder, *Washington Post*, March 31, 1998.

23 Conason and Lyons, *The Hunting Of The President*, pp. 259-264.

24 "Pressgate" Steven Brill, *Brill's Content*, p. 127.

25 "Reno Has Bungled the Lewinsky Case" Thomas Oliphant, *Boston Globe*, June 30, 1998.

26 "Pressgate" *Brill's Content*, p.127.

27 *Ibid*, p. 128.

28 Conason and Lyons, *The Hunting Of The President*, pp. 356-357.

29 *Ibid*, p. 127.

30 Ibid, pp. 356-357; Brock, *Blinded By the Right*, p. 317.

31 Brock, *Blinded By the Right*, p. 317.

32 Toobin, *A Vast Conspiracy*, p. 202.

33 "Reno Has Bungled the Lewinsky Case" *Boston Globe*.

34 Woodward, Bob, *Shadow: Five Presidents and the Legacy of Watergate*, Simon and Schuster, 1999, p. 516.

35 Sam Dash's November 20, 1998 letter to Kenneth Starr; Blumenthal, *The Clinton Wars*, pp. 518-519.

36 Blumenthal, *The Clinton Wars*, pp. 484, 539, 587-588.

37 "U.S. Never Had Firm Grasp on Terrorism" Judith Miller, Jeff Gerth and Don Van Natta Jr., *New York Times*.

38 E-mail from Zoe Lofgren, Member of Congress, to *MoveOn*, February 12, 1999.

39 Baker, Peter (of the *Washington Post*), *The Breach: Inside the Impeachment and Trial of William Jefferson Clinton,* Simon and Schuster, 2000, p. 204.

40 *Ibid*, p. 16.

41 Ibid, pp. 252, 263.

42 Ibid, pp. 43-44.

43 Ibid, pp. 16, 138, 231-232.

44 Blumenthal, *The Clinton Wars*, pp. 537-539.

45 Woodward, *Shadow: Five Presidents and the Legacy of Watergate*, pp. 484-489.

46 "Grass-Roots Organizing Effort Gets a Big Boost from Internet" Melissa Healy, *Los Angeles Times*, January 13, 1999.

47 *Censure* and *MoveOn*, press release, December 15, 1998.

48 Original *MoveOn* website.

49 Toobin, *A Vast Conspiracy*, p. 334.

50 *Ibid*, p. 333.

51 Blumenthal, *The Clinton Wars*, pp. 490-504.

52 "Criminal? Possibly, Impeachable? No" Herman Schwartz, *Los Angeles Times*.

53 Letter from Zoe Lofgren to *MoveOn*, February 10, 1999.

54 "Criminal? Possibly, Impeachable? No" *Los Angeles Times*.

55 Conason and Lyons, *The Hunting Of The President*, pp. 370-371.

56 "Kenneth Starr says he shouldn't have been involved in the Lewinsky case" *Associated Press*, December 2, 2004; "Rep. Hyde reflects on 30 years of office" *Andy Shaw, ABC7, Chicago.com*, April 22, 2005.

57 "DeLay to Be Subject of Ethics Complaint" Charles Babington, *Washington Post*, June 15, 2004. The following are additional articles on DeLay's ethics:

"GOP Comes Around to Majority View" Andrea Stone and William M. Welch, *USA Today*, June 17, 2004;

"Tom DeLay's Amoral Code" Katrina vanden Heuvel, *The Nation*, June 23, 2005;

"Ethics committee awaits DeLay's response," Rachna Sheth, *The Daily Texan*, July 2, 2004;

"DeLay's Corporate Fundraising Investigated" Jeffrey Smith, *Washington Post*, July 12, 2005;

"Curbing GOP's iron rule in Congress" Marty Meehan, *boston.com*, July 16, 2004;

"House rejects outside probe of majority leader" *Associated Press*, October 9, 2004;

"GOP should ask DeLay to quit leadership post" Editorial Board, *statesman.com*, October 10, 2004;

"Breaking News...DeLay Gets Served!" Jesselee, *The Stateholder*, October 21, 2004;

"House Ethics Panel in Gridlock" Mike Allen, *Washington Post,* March 11, 2005;

"DeLay And Company" Karen Tumulty, *Times Online Edition*, March 14, 2005;

"Defiant DeLay Dirty Dealings" *The Center for American Progress/Progress Report,* March 16, 2005.

58 "Get Personal, Mrs. Clinton" Richard Cohen, *Washington Post*.

Book Sources

Baker, Peter (of the *Washington Post*), *The Breach: Inside the Impeachment and Trial of William Jefferson Clinton*, Simon and Schuster, 2000.

Blumenthal, Sidney, *The Clinton Wars*, Farrar, Strauss and Giroux, 2003.

Brock, David, *Blinded By the Right: The Conscience of an Ex-Conservative*, Crown Publishers, 2002.

Conason, Joe and Lyons, Gene, *The Hunting Of The President: The Ten-Year Campaign to Destroy Bill and Hillary Clinton*, St. Martin's Press, 2000.

Toobin, Jeffrey, *A Vast Conspiracy*, Touchstone, 2000.

Woodward, Bob, *Shadow: Five Presidents and the Legacy of Watergate*, Simon and Schuster, 1999.

Chapter Three

New Far Right Agenda Ignores Terrorism

"Obviously, Republicans were not going to let Democrats say what needed to be said....But since the facts could not be ignored or suppressed, they reported them without drawing certain obvious, not to mention devastating, conclusions."

—John Dean, Find Law's Legal Commentary on the Republican-led Joint Congressional Inquiry into 9/11.

July 29, 2003

As the Clinton administration was winding down, the far right chose George W. Bush as its candidate for the presidency in 2001—a governor, with name recognition, and a "regular guy" image who made friends easily. Records were set in raising funds for his campaign. Early in the primaries, however, the popular

Senator McCain won a convincing victory over Bush. The far right did not waste any time. Using their signature brand of politics of personal destruction, they destroyed McCain in short order.

In the general election, former Vice-President Al Gore received more of the popular vote than Bush, while Bush eked out an Electoral College victory. A Florida recount might have swung the election to Gore. Among those strongly opposed to the recount was Tom DeLay who sent people to Florida to interfere with and stop it. Joining them in Florida was John Bolton, the President's controversial nominee for UN Ambassador. This contentious matter finally ended up in the Supreme Court. Led by far-right justices, the Court handed down a 5-4 decision not to complete the recount in progress, in effect appointing President Bush.

We move on to the new Bush administration, with the far right now firmly in charge. Their vendetta against President Clinton had diverted the nation from the major threat of global terrorism and al-Qaeda. We will see how, in their haste to move quickly on the far-right agenda, the Bush administration left the nation totally unprepared for the al-Qaeda threat—resulting in the worst U.S. disaster in history. President Bush and his key advisors failed to respond to:

- An al-Qaeda declaration of war on the United States, a history of previous al-Qaeda attacks, and top expert advice that this terrorist network was the gravest and most immediate threat to our nation.

- Strong urgings to deal with that threat and strengthen homeland security from (1) both Clinton's and the President's own administrations and (2) two bipartisan commissions, one on national security and the other on terrorism.

- An unprecedented surge of warnings during the spring and summer that a major catastrophe was about to befall our nation. This included the possibility of using hijacked commercial aircraft as weapons.

From his very first day in office the President did not give the al-Qaeda threat serious attention. Later, as the threats surged and became more menacing, he did not take sensible precautions to prevent the attacks. Gross neglect of the threat and failure to prepare for it had two major consequences (1) our nation was left completely vulnerable to attack and (2) the 9/11 terrorists had a greatly increased chance of success.

Following the disaster, the President evaded any responsibility and strongly opposed an investigative commission. Instead, his Administration conducted a massive cover-up, allowing others to bear the brunt of the President's mistakes.

Pressured by the 9/11 families, Congress eventually created

the 9/11 Commission. The Commission commented extensively on 9/11 responsibility at lower levels of government and in Congress, but omitted the very top ones in the Executive Branch. Because of the approaching presidential elections, the Commission believed a partisan fight within the Commission and a report lacking unity would threaten acceptance of its recommendations for a more secure America.

Response to Terrorist Attacks During the Clinton Years

The first attack on the New York World Trade Center occurred in late 1993. It killed six individuals and injured hundreds more. Osama bin Laden's name eventually surfaced in the investigation which resulted in some of his sympathizers being sent to prison.[1] Then in 1996, terrorists bombed a U. S. military complex in Saudi Arabia, killing nineteen Americans. In the same year bin Laden declared a holy war against Americans for occupying Saudi Arabia.[2]

In late 1998 bin Laden again announced a declaration of war and bombed two of our embassies, killing 224 people and injuring about 5,000.

During the 1990s there was no public or congressional groundswell of support for military action against terrorism. As discussed in Chapter 2, the House of Representatives was pre-occupied with destroying the Clinton presidency, and the Senate got bogged down in the resulting impeachment trial. Nevertheless, the Clinton Administration did increase anti-terrorism budgets, launched cruise missiles at al-Qaeda training camps, and tried several times to capture or kill their leader, Osama bin Laden, and his senior lieutenants.[3] As part of these efforts, President Clinton authorized the CIA to assassinate bin Laden. In addition, he received a pipeline of daily reports on al-Qaeda activities and exercised extreme precautions at the turn of the century to prevent further attacks.

Just before the 2000 U.S. presidential elections, terrorists struck yet again with a suicide attack on the *U.S.S. Cole*, killing seventeen U.S. military service personnel and injuring many more. This prompted the Clinton administration to prepare a bold plan of attack against al-Qaeda. However, Clinton decided he couldn't start a war without proof of bin Laden's responsibility for the *Cole* attack—especially since that war would have to be conducted by a new administration. So his plan was passed on to the new Administration in special briefings with Vice-President Richard Cheney and National Security Advisor Condoleezza Rice. According to an unnamed senior Bush official, the Clinton plan contained all the steps that were eventually taken after 9/11.[4]

Bush Administration Fails to Heed Warnings

As noted, when the Bush administration first took office, al-Qaeda was already a major threat to our nation.

The President *was warned at the outset* that al-Qaeda would be his "greatest" and "gravest" threat. This advice came directly from President Clinton and CIA Director George Tenet. Despite these warnings, the White House counter-terrorism unit was soon downgraded and no longer had access to the President or to agency heads.[5] Additionally, in response to a powerful banking lobby, the new Administration abandoned a global crackdown on terrorist funding.

Paul Bremer, who later took charge in Iraq, chaired a National Commission on Terrorism which rendered its report several months before Bush took office. Subsequently, in late February 2001, Bremer said that the Bush administration is:

> "...paying no attention to the problem of terrorism. What they will do is stagger along until there's a major incident and then suddenly say, 'Oh my God, shouldn't we be organized to deal with this?'....They've been given a window of opportunity...and they're not taking advantage of it."[6]

At about the same time, a bipartisan Congressional commission on U.S. National Security, assembled by Clinton and Congress, reported that the United States was vulnerable to catastrophic attack by terrorists. In White House meetings, the Commission Chair argued for the report's major recommendation—a National Homeland Security Agency. Bush rejected it.[7]

During the spring of 2001 terrorism warnings increased dramatically and, by that summer, they had reached a crescendo. Before 9/11 the President received 40 individual CIA briefings mentioning al-Qaeda and/or bin Laden. In the now infamous briefing in Texas on August 6, 2001, the CIA told the President about al-Qaeda's determination "to attack within the United States."[8] They said that al-Qaeda had operatives residing in the U.S. and that the FBI found "patterns of suspicious activity consistent with preparations for hijacking." The CIA considered the August 6 briefing an opportunity to tell the President that the bin Laden threat was "both current and serious."[9] The President did not take control, call agency heads together, or go into a crisis mode. He did not warn the public.

Vice-President Dick Cheney *also received special briefings* (1) from White House terrorism experts on the gravity of the al-Qaeda threat and (2) from the CIA, confirming al-Qaeda's responsibility for the *U.S.S. Cole* attack. During his campaign Bush had said "there must be consequences" for the *U.S.S. Cole*. Now in charge, he did not respond with military action or resume covert actions of the Clinton administration.

In midsummer, Cheney, the President, and his national security aides all received classified briefings, showing that already high threats had surged even higher. Their briefings included such headlines as "Bin Laden Threats Are Real" and "Bin Laden Planning High Profile Attacks."[10]

Cheney had been asked to oversee a "national effort" to respond to domestic attacks. However, the focus of his efforts was on state-funded terrorists using weapons of mass destruction. No mention was made of bin Laden or al-Qaeda. A report was due to Congress by October 1. By September 11, Cheney's task force had barely gotten underway; there was no chance of meeting the October 1 deadline.

National Security Advisor Condoleezza Rice *determined the agenda* for National Security meetings, which the President and other top key members attended. She also had responsibility for interagency coordination on national security matters. At transition time she too received special briefings and other information on the severity of the al-Qaeda threat.

In late January, 2001, Richard Clarke, who was in charge of counterterrorism at the White House, "urgently" requested that she set up a cabinet-level meeting on the al-Qaeda threat. He said there were al-Qaeda cells in the United States and that we would make a major error if we "underestimated" the threat.[11] No meeting was held. Clarke's briefing to Rice included the Clinton plan to remove the al-Qaeda network. As *Time Magazine*'s "Secret History" points out, that plan became a victim of "not invented here," turf wars, and time spent on pet policies of top Bush officials.[12]

In June, 2001, CIA Director Tenet sent Rice an intelligence summary and met with her personally. Among other things, he reported: "It is highly likely that a significant al-Qaeda attack is in the near future, within several weeks." He added: "Most of the al-Qaeda network is anticipating an attack....Based on a review of all source reporting over the last five months, we believe that [bin Laden] will launch a significant attack against U.S. and/or Israeli interests in the coming weeks. The attack will be spectacular and designed to inflict mass casualties....Attack preparations have been made. Attack will occur with little or no warning." According to Tenet, "....this is going to be a big one."[13]

A national security meeting on terrorism was not held until three months later in September. On September 11, Rice was supposed to give a speech on "the threats and problems of today and the day after, not the world of yesterday." The speech promoted missile defense—the far right's new priority—and contained no mention of either bin Laden or al-Qaeda. The speech, of course, was never given.

Much later, the 9/11 Commission asked Rice about the still classified August 6th presidential briefing memo. Under oath, she mislead the Commission, saying the memo was mostly "historic."[14]

Defense Secretary Donald Rumsfeld and Deputy Paul Wolfowitz *were obsessed* with a new missile defense system. In a meeting with the deputies of other agencies, Wolfowitz said: "I just don't understand why we are beginning by talking about this one man, bin Laden" and "Who cares about a little terrorist in Afghanistan."[15] Meanwhile, Secretary Rumsfeld threatened a presidential veto if Congress shifted $600 million of his missile-shield money to counterterrorism.

During the first national security meeting on terrorism in September, Rumsfeld appeared more interested in Iraq. His key position in charge of counterterrorism at DOD had not been filled yet. Rumsfeld acknowledged to the Commission that his Department was focused on other issues. Confirming this, the Commission learned (1) the Department had no mission to counter al-Qaeda and (2) according to the Joint Chiefs Chairman, the Administration "did not show much interest in military options."[16]

Attorney General John Ashcroft *laid out his priorities* for the FBI in February 2001—counterterrorism was missing. In May, Ashcroft set forth seven major goals for his Department. Again, counterterrorism was missing. In July, Ashcroft was briefed by the CIA and FBI on the severity of the al-Qaeda threat. In early September, Ashcroft flatly rejected a $50 million request for the FBI's counterterrorism program. According to the FBI, he asked *not to be briefed on this subject again.*[17]

The attitude and priorities of Bush's chief advisors and department heads on the threat of terrorism can only reflect that of the President himself. The *Washington Post* concluded that the Bush administration "gave scant attention to an adversary whose lethal ambitions and savvy had been well understood for years."

Warnings Could Not Get Any Worse

The 9/11 Commission Report chapter, "The System is Blinking Red," shows that the number and severity of reported threats were unparalleled and that many officials knew something terrible was planned. Warnings were in terms of "catastrophic proportions" and "on a calamitous level, causing the world to be in turmoil." Nearly frantic with concern, the CIA Director repeatedly warned the White House of a "significant attack in the near future." In an August 2001 speech to a terrorism convention, his head of counterterrorism said: "We are going to be struck soon, many Americans are going to die, and it could be in the U.S."[18]

The warnings were described as the "most urgent in decades." Desperate to get top level attention, the White House Chief of Counterterrorism, Richard Clarke, asked top "decision makers to imagine a future day when hundreds of Americans lay dead."[19] In another instance, two officials in government considered resigning in order to go public with their concerns. The head of the FBI's national security for New

York City *did* resign in frustration two weeks before 9/11. He took a position in charge of security at the World Trade Center—and did not survive the attack.[20]

During the unprecedented surge of threat information, countries around the world tried to alert the U.S. to the danger at least 15 times. These countries are identified in the chart on the next four pages, along with highlights of their warnings.[21] The chart is not complete because the Administration refused to declassify all information bearing on the 9/11 threat.

The Bush administration, and in particular National Security Advisor Rice, claimed no one had ever considered that terrorists might use airplanes as weapons. The evidence of record shows otherwise. As depicted in the following chart, the Joint Intelligence Committee investigation into 9/11, and others, found numerous indications of plans through August 2001 to use airplanes as weapons, including interest by bin Laden in using commercial pilots as terrorists.

Ed Asner and Burt Hall

When	Source	Warning Highlight
1998	CIA Intelligence Source	Fly explosive-laden plane into World Trade Center
1999	Report to Nat'l Intelligence Council	bin Laden might crash plane into Pentagon, White House, or CIA Headquarters
March 2001	Italy	Warns of "very, very, secret" al-Qaeda plan
April 2001	Afghanistan	Warns of al-Qaeda plot to attack U.S. in suicide missions involving aircraft
June 2001	Germany	Warns of plans to hijack commercial aircraft to use as weapons
May-July 2001	National Security Agency	Intercepted at least thirty-three communications about impending attack

74

Misuse of Power

When	Source	Warning Highlight
July 2001	Great Britain	Warns al-Qaeda is in "the final stages" of preparing a terrorist attack
July 2001	Afghanistan	Taliban Foreign Minister warns of huge attack on America
July 2001	Argentina	Relays warning of an attack of major proportions
July 2001	Egypt	Warns that 20 al-Qaeda members have slipped into U.S. and 4 of them have received flight training
Late Summer 2001	Jordan	Warns that aircraft will be used in major attack inside U.S.
1994-August 2001	Congressional Intelligence Committee	12 examples of intelligence data—possible use of planes as weapons (may include some above)

When	Source	Warning Highlight
August 2001	Morocco	bin Laden plans "large scale operations in summer or fall,"—disappointed 1993 World Trade attack failed
August 2001	Russia	Putin warns that suicide pilots are training for attacks on U.S. targets
August 2001	Persia	Warns "spectacular terrorist operation" to take place soon
August 2001	Great Britain	Warns of multiple airplane hijackings—warning said to have reached Bush
August 2001	Egypt	Warns that al-Qaeda in advanced stages of planning significant attack on U.S.

When	Source	Warning Highlight
August 2001	Israel	Warns "major assault on the U.S." imminent; gives CIA terrorist list of persons living in U.S.; 4 actual hijackers on list
August 2001	France	Passes on Israeli warning (above)
Summer 2001	CIA Director	Repeatedly warns White House of "significant attack in near future"

President Doesn't Even Try to Defend Against Attack

During the presidential transition there were no problems of continuity in the Bush administration regarding terrorism. Clinton's Chief of Counterterrorism (Richard Clarke) became Bush's Chief, Clinton's CIA Director (Tenet) became Bush's Director, and an al-Qaeda attack plan was already available— the one that was used *after 9/11*.

The threat was real and possible targets were known; only the timing was uncertain. Taken individually, the threat information was disturbing but, taken collectively, the information was overpowering. Exact knowledge of the targets to be hit or the timing was not really required. *All the Administration had to do was protect against the hijacking of commercial aircraft—just that one thing.* Yet, nothing was done to fix airline vulnerabilities or prepare for suicide hijacking. As the 9/11 Commission concluded, domestic agencies never mobilized a response, got direction, or had a plan. The public was not warned.

It is hard to imagine why the President did not demonstrate greater concern and take responsible action. For example, a preemptive strike on al-Qaeda would have been more than justified by bin Laden's declaration of war, his four previous attacks, and the near-frenzy warnings of new ones. As to defensive measures, Bush did not direct Agency heads to neutralize the most likely attack—commercial aircraft hijackings.

These things didn't happen before September 11—and we still haven't been told why.

The people of the United States needed to be highly aware, observant, and proactive. Presidential leadership would have stimulated a new level of energy, creativity, and cooperation within federal and local agencies that would have also elicited maximum public participation. With reenergized government surveillance and public participation, the country would have been much better prepared to avert the horrible tragedy. It's even possible that the disaster could have been avoided if the President had maintained the priority of the previous administration, retaliated against al-Qaeda for the *U.S.S. Cole* attack, mobilized Homeland Security protection, and responded in a serious way to the extraordinary warnings during the spring and summer of 2001.

What was the President's problem? Was he preoccupied with his own agenda? Was he worried about the impact of public fear of terrorism on a sagging economy? Did he downgrade concerns of the previous administration? Did he get poor advice? *Time Magazine*'s "The Secret History" concluded that the disaster wasn't averted "because 2001 saw a systematic collapse in the ability of Washington's national security apparatus to handle the terrorist threat."

The 9/11 Cover-up

The President's attitude on cooperation with the 9/11 Commission was just the opposite of what it should have been. As Commander in Chief, he should have worked closely with the Commission to get at the heart of the problem, with the idea of preventing future attacks. Instead, for a year, the White House consistently blocked the investigative commission and then stonewalled it for another year.

As the Commissioners themselves have acknowledged, they suffered from lengthy delays, maddening restrictions, and disputes over access to sensitive documents and witnesses. As just one example, the Commission (after months of denial) finally got *limited* access to Bush's intelligence briefings, but only after threatening him with a subpoena.[22]

Politics Influences the Commission Report

The Commission's report has excellent findings on and recommendations for the intelligence community, FBI, immigration, Congress, etc.— but, no findings on the White House, its priorities, or presidential leadership. Why didn't the Commission connect the dots?

The five Republican and five Democratic members of the 9/11 Commission were faced with an enormously difficult situation during an election year—either (1) don't address top-level responsibility and come out with a unified, bipartisan report that would surely be acted upon or (2) assign some responsibility to the President and his advisors and have a divided and contentious report that would gather dust. The Commission firmly believed that "in order to have a strong public impact the report had to be unanimous."

1. **Was 9/11 Preventable?** The Commission says opportunities were missed, but all those mentioned were at the operational level—none at top levels of government.[23]

The fact is the President did not attempt to reduce a known high-level threat or the nation's vulnerability to it, nor did he respond to expert advice and frantic warnings of imminent attacks. Any one or a combination of these actions could have prevented 9/11.

2. **Did the President Understand the Threat?** The Commission says the President did not have a complete picture of the threat or an understanding of its gravity.[24]

The fact is the President did have a full understanding of the threat and its gravity, as explained in *Time Magazine*'s "Secret History," Richard Clarke's book, *Against All Enemies*, and the Commission's Report itself. For example, the Commission's Report chapter, "The System is Blinking Red," discloses compelling evidence of an impending catastrophic attack which demanded *immediate* presidential action.

3. **Who was Responsible?** The Commission says senior officials across government share in the responsibility and that our national leaders could have done more. It lays much of the blame on intelligence, FBI, immigration, Congress, etc.[25]

The fact is our national leaders should have reduced the threat and our nation's vulnerability to it. Senior officials across government surely would have been much more responsive to the threat had the President led the way, called in the heads of *their* agencies and shared his threat information with *them* and the *general public*.

The Commission's failure to assess any top level responsibility has already been challenged by two book reviews of its report, and by Richard Clarke in a *New York Times* Op-Ed piece. Clarke served three presidents in the White House, including Bush, as the counterterrorism czar. He concluded that the Bush administration did not take the threat seriously and squandered the opportunity to eliminate al-Qaeda. He added that by going to Iraq "...we are not doing what is necessary to make America safe from that threat." Reaching a similar conclusion, David Ignatius of the *Washington Post* wrote:

"The Bush team...didn't get serious about bin Laden...In truth, nothing would have prevented the national security advisor...from mobilizing anti-terrorism policy against al-Qaeda in the months before 9/11. That's what makes this story a tragedy—that existing institutions of government might have averted the disaster, if they had taken action."

In a lengthy analysis of the Commission report in *The New York Review of Books*, involving interviews with both commissioners and key staff members, Elizabeth Drew concluded:

"In an effort to achieve a unanimous, bipartisan report, the Commission decided not to assign 'individual blame' and avoided overt criticism of the President himself. Still, the report is a powerful indictment of the Bush administration for its behavior before and after the attack of September 11."

The Paralysis in the Commission's Analysis

The Commission focused on a question too narrow and nearly impossible to answer: Could 9/11 have been prevented?

To answer that question either way would have been construed as self-serving and encouraged the use of 20/20 hindsight.

The broader, more appropriate question is to put yourself in the shoes of the President during the months leading up to 9/11. What would a reasonable and prudent person do in the same situation—irrespective of the result? In other words: What would any president do when confronted with an al-Qaeda declaration of war, a history of earlier attacks, strong advice on the gravity of the threat, and serious warnings of an impending attack?

It would be nice to know exactly where the new attacks might take place and their exact timing. However, the only reasonable alternative for any thinking president would have been to put the country in a crisis mode and take immediate action to protect the nation—especially commercial aircraft. In the end, the measures taken should have shown a government in action, anxious to protect its people and determined to make it difficult for terrorist attacks to succeed. That's all we can expect—*but no less.*

As the book, *The Terror Timeline*, so succinctly points out, "The public record reflects that the extreme focus on terrorism in place at the end of the Clinton administration dropped dramatically under the Bush administration. With few exceptions, little attention was paid to terrorism, even as the number of warnings reached unprecedented levels."

The Bottom Line

President Bush presided over the greatest national security failure in our history. We may never know for an absolute certainty whether 9/11 could have been prevented. The critical issue is Bush's inattention to the subject, his lack of response to repeated warnings, his absence of leadership when it really counted, and the White House cover-up since then.

The failure of the Administration to respond to the *U.S.S. Cole* attack, as Bush campaigned he would, was a serious mistake. When terrorists perceive that the United States is weak, they are emboldened to strike again.

Although the politically-divided Commission on 9/11 could not bring itself to assess responsibility at the very top level, the information is there in its report for anyone who wants to read the facts and draw their own conclusions. When the report was released, the scapegoats came from lower ranks and middle management. Top management must have breathed a huge sigh of relief.

There was a serious lack of presidential leadership before 9/11. Unfortunately the brunt of the responsibility fell on the intelligence agencies, FBI, and immigration. Unless the official record is corrected, we will lose an important lesson in national leadership and accountability at the very highest level of government.

Had Bush prevented the 9/11 attacks, terrorism would not be the number one issue it is today. He didn't prevent the attacks and his neglect of the issue actually helped him get reelected. Ironically, leadership on terror was one of the key reasons. He chose New York City, a Democratic citadel, to host the Republican Convention near Ground Zero. The slogan was "Stay Safe: Reelect Bush."

The most incredible thing is that President Bush has exploited a national tragedy for personal gain with no account-ability. He used it to support a war in Iraq, to gain control of Congress, and to further his own reelection campaign.

Endnotes

1   "U.S. never had firm grip on terrorism" Judith Miller, Jeff Gerth and Don Van Natta Jr., *New York Times*.

2   "The Secret History" *Time Magazine*, August 12, 2002, p. 32.

3   "Broad Effort Launched After '98 Attack" Barton Gellman, *Washington Post*, December 19, 2001.

4   "The Secret History" *Time Magazine*, August 12, 2002, p. 31; "9/11 and a Lack of Presidential Leadership" Burt Hall, *The Humanist*, March/April 2003.

5   Clarke, Richard A., *Against All Enemies*, Free Press, 2004, p. 230.

6   "In early '01, Bremer Bashed Bush on Terror" Kevin Featherly, *Kevlog Archive*, April 29, 2004. (Paul Bremmer chaired the congressionally created National Commission on Terrorism and issued his report in June 2000. There is no evidence of a meaningful response by the Executive Branch.) See also: Thompson, Paul, *The Terror Timeline*, Regan Books, 2004, p. 90.

7   "We Predicted It" Jake Tapper, *Salon*, September 12, 2001.

8   "The System Is Blinking Red" *The 9/11 Commission Report,* 2004.

9   *Ibid.*

10 Ibid.

11 Ibid.

12 "The Secret History" *Time Magazine*, August 12, 2002.

13 "The System Is Blinking Red" *The 9/11 Commission Report.*

14 *Ibid.*

15 Clarke, *Against All Enemies*, p. 231.

16 "The System Is Blinking Red" *The 9/11 Commission Report.*

17 *Ibid.*

18 Ibid.

19 Ibid.

20 "The Secret History" *Time Magazine*, August 12, 2002, p. 43.

21 Thompson, Paul, *The Terror Timeline*, Regan Books, 2004; "9/11 and a Lack of Presidential Leadership" Burt Hall, *The Humanist*, March/April 2003.

22 "9/11 Panel Threatens to Issue Subpoena for Bush's Briefings" *New York Times*, February 10, 2004. Below are other articles dealing with the White House cover-up;

"White House refuses to release September 11 info" *Knight Ridder Newspapers*, May 5, 2003;

"White House keeps secrets to hide failure, Graham says" *Palm Beach Post*, 2003;

"Sept. 11 panel criticizes White House" *Los Angeles Times*, July 9, 2003;

"Why does 9/11 inquiry scare Bush" *The Berkshire Eagle*, July 12, 2003;

"Sept. 11 panel leader warns White House of subpoenas" *The New York Times*, October 26, 2003;

"Stonewalling the 9/11 Commission" *Wall Street Journal*, July 8, 2003; *Washington Post,* September 24, 2003; *New York Times*, October 26 and November 8, 2003;

"9/11 Panel Seeks More Documents From White House" *Washington Post*, September 24, 2003;

"9/11 Panel May Reject Offer of Limited Access to Briefings" *New York Times*, November 7, 2003;

"Sept. 11 panelists, victim's families rip document deal" *New York Times*, November 14, 2003;

"The 9/11 Cover-up" *AlterNet.org*, November 21, 2003;

9/11 family statement re: Commission access to sensitive documents and conflict of interest, December 2, 2003;

"What's Bush Hiding from 9/11 Commission" *Working for Change*, January 22, 2004;

"Sept. 11 Commission Faces Fight Over Deadline Extension" *Gov Exec*, January 21, 2004;

"White House Holding Notes Taken by 9/11 Commission" *Washington Post*, January 31, 2004;

"The White House: A New Fight Over Sept. 11" *Newsweek*, February 10, 2004;

"9/11 Panel to Accept Summary of Briefings" *Washington Post*, February 11, 2004;

"Failure of 9/11 Commission to Subpoena the White House" *Voices of September 11 Newsletter*, February 11, 2004;

"Bush Plays Bait-and-Switch with 9/11 Panel" *Newsday.com*, February 19, 2004;

Statement of 9/11 Families on commission access to presidential daily briefings, extension of its deadline and request for Senate hearings on progress, February 20, 2004.

23 9/11 Commission Executive Summary.

24 *Ibid.*

25 Ibid.

Other Sources

"The Secrets of September 11" *MSNBC.com*, May 1, 2003.

"Terror Commission Seeks Classified Papers" *Associated Press,* February 28, 2003.

"Why keep Americans guessing about 9/11?" *Sacramento Bee*, May 16, 2003.

"Classified: Censoring the Report About 9/11?" *Newsweek*, June 2, 2003.

"9/11 Report Cites Intelligence Failures" *Associated Press*, July 24, 2003.

"The 9/11 Report Raises More Questions about the White House Statements on Intelligence" John Dean, *Find Law's Legal Commentary*, July 29, 2003.

"Where the Blame Lies" *Intervention Magazine*, December 11, 2003.

"Clarke blaming Bush for not taking precautions before World Trade Center attack" *Foster's/Citizen Online*, December 11, 2003.

"Condi and the 9/11 Commission" *Time Online Edition*, December 23, 2003.

"September 11: Will Terror Panel's Report Be an Election Issue?" *Newsweek*, January 14, 2004.

"Bush agrees to New 9/11 Commission Deadline" *Associated Press,* February 5, 2004.

Voices of September 11 Newsletter, February 9, 2004.

"White House Noncommittal on Testimony" *Palm Beach Post*, February 13, 2004.

"President Agrees to Meet (Part of) Panel Privately About September 11 Attacks" *Palm Beach Post*, February 14, 2004.

"Investigating the Investigation" *AlterNet.org*, February 17, 2004.

"Weak on Terror" *New York Times*, March 16, 2004.

"Bush and 9/11: What We Need to Know" *Time Magazine*, March 17, 2004.

Statement of 9/11 families on Condoleezza Rice Testimony, March 30, 2004.

"9/11 Widows" *New York Times*, April 1, 2004.

"Uneven Response Seen on Terror in Summer of 2001" *New York Times*, April 4, 2004.

"Declassified Memo Said al-Qaeda Was in U.S." *Washington Post*, April 10, 2004.

"The Texas Try on Terrorism" *Center For American Progress*, April 12, 2004.

"The 9/11 Investigation: Bending Reality" *St. Louis Post Dispatch*, April 12, 2004.

"Will Bush Own Up?" *Washington Post*, April 13, 2004.

"Panel Says Bush Saw Repeated Warnings" *Washington Post*, April 14, 2004.

"9/11 Files Show Warnings Were Urgent and Persistent" *New York Times*, April 18, 2004.

"The Wrong Debate on Terrorism" Richard Clarke, *New York Times*, April 25, 2004.

"Will The Commissioners Cave?" *Tom Paine Common Sense,* June 21, 2004.

"Report on 9/11 to be released this month" *Knight Ridder*, July 10, 2004.

"The Book on Terror" Reviewed by David Ignatius, *Washington Post*, July 30, 2004.

"Correcting the record on 9/11" *New York Times.*

"9/11 Panel Roiling Campaign Platforms" *Washington Post*, August 9, 2004.

"9/11 Assessment Again Shows Lost Personal Responsibility" *The Boston Channel*, August 10, 2004.

"We could have stopped him" *Guardian Unlimited*, August 10, 2004.

"Former CIA Agent Says Bush to Blame for 9/11" *Common Dreams,* September 22, 2004.

"Pinning the Blame" Elizabeth Drew, *The New York Review of Books*, September 23, 2004.

"Edwards Accuses Bush of Exploiting 9/11" *Associated Press*, October 18, 2004.

"The 9/11 Secret in the CIA's Back Pocket" *Los Angeles Times*, October 19, 2004.

"Evolving Nature of al-Qaeda Is Misunderstood Critic Says" *New York Times,* November 8, 2004.

"'01 Memo to Rice Warned of al-Qaeda and Offered Plan" Scott Shane, *New York Times*, February 12, 2005.

"Bush team tried to suppress pre-9/11 report into al-Qaeda" Andrew Buncombe, *The Independent*, February 11, 2005.

Chapter Four

Far Right Capitalizes On 9/11 To Launch Unnecessary War

"In terms of the fight against terror, the war in Iraq has been a big loss. We've energized the enemy. We've wasted the talents of many men and women who fought bravely and tenaciously in Iraq. Thousands upon thousands of American men and women have lost arms and legs, or been paralyzed or horribly burned or killed in this ill-advised war. A wiser administration would have avoided that carnage and marshaled instead a more robust effort against Al Qaeda, which remains a deadly threat to America."

—Bob Herbert, *New York Times*, Feb. 21, 2005

The Bush administration did not take the terror threat seriously or take precautionary measures to protect the nation. After a stumbling start, the President did pull the country together and respond aggressively, but his response didn't last. He and his far-right advisors spent a year planning to invade a country that had nothing to do with 9/11 or al-Qaeda and was not even a threat to the United States. Al-Qaeda continues to attack around the world and is still a threat to the United States.

When he sought authority to use force, the President promised Congress and the American people that he would not engage in war, except as a last resort. He did not fulfill that promise. Using threat information known to be inherently uncertain, the President and his far-right advisors misled the American people by presenting it as absolute fact. At the same time, the Administration dismissed findings of international weapons experts on the ground in Iraq. These inspectors were not asked to check out U.S. intelligence and the President did not send our own weapons experts in to participate in the inspection process. The fact is the President and his advisors were already on a path to war and used intelligence to suit their own needs.

Had the President taken normal precautions, it would have been evident before the war that (1) U.S. intelligence was faulty, (2) the Administration's assertions to Congress and the public about the threat were incorrect, and (3) these assertions were being disproved by inspectors on the ground in Iraq.

Invading Iraq has weakened the war on terror, and the President has no realistic exit strategy. His approach to the war on terror has been too narrow and limited in scope to solve a global problem. In subsequent sections of this chapter you will find:

- Options that were available to the President other than war.

- A more appropriate way for Congress to have authorized the use of force.

- Two ways to exit Iraq with honor.

- A broad strategy designed to eventually end the threat of global terrorism.

Impending War Influences Intelligence

Initial success of the President's response to 9/11 soon evaporated with his detour to war in Iraq. Vice-President Cheney had served both in Congress and in several administrations, including positions as White House Chief of Staff and Secretary of Defense. He knew first hand that threat assessments are based on estimates and assumptions, sometimes using questionable sources. Yet, both he and the President presented this information over and over again to the public with absolute certainty.

The President did not do the responsible thing—simply have our intelligence data checked out by the 250 international inspectors who were on the ground in Iraq. The inspectors (representing 60 countries) were experts on each WMD category, had no axe to grind, and were in a position to obtain the actual facts. Intelligence used by the White House to promote the war was being tested and disproved during 700 UN inspections at 500 sites.[1] Our own experts were invited to participate in the inspections, but the Administration did not respond. Inspections ended in early March 2003 when they were preempted by Bush's decision to go to war.

As Bob Woodward describes in detail in his book, *Plan of Attack*, Bush had decided on a path to war *more than a year* before the invasion. A photo in Woodward's book shows the President meeting with General Tommy Franks in Crawford, Texas on Dec. 28, 2001, for a "war planning session on Iraq." At Bush's direction, the CIA participated in this war planning and sent a team to northern Iraq to lay the groundwork for the invasion. To arrange for covert entry, CIA Director Tenet personally went there in March 2002 and told Kurd leaders that the United States was serious—the military and the CIA were coming.

In mid-2002, President Bush shifted $700 million from the Afghanistan war to preparations for war in Iraq. At the same time, a secret Downing Street meeting in England took place on recent discussions with Washington:

- Military action was inevitable—Bush had made up his mind.

- Intelligence and facts were being fixed around that policy.

- Military action would begin next January.

- The case was thin—Saddam was not threatening his neighbors and his WMD capability was less than Lybia, North Korea, and Iran.

- The White House had no patience with the UN route.

- There was little discussion of the aftermath after military action.

- Prime Minister Blair concluded that it would make a big difference politically and legally if Saddam refused to let the inspectors back in.

—"The Secret Downing Street Memo" David Manning, *The Sunday Times-Britain*, May 1, 2005.

During the summer and fall of 2002, Administration officials began referring to ominous Iraqi threats, linked Iraq to al-Qaeda, and ventured the possibility of another catastrophe like 9/11. The result was a policy-based decision that drove the intelligence, rather than the other way around. Adding to this pressure, the White House gave the CIA only three weeks to prepare an October 2002 National Intelligence Estimate for Congress to authorize the use of force.

People inside the CIA were "disheartened, dispirited, and angry." One senior CIA official put it this way, "Information not consistent with the Administration agenda was discarded and information that was [consistent] was not seriously scrutinized." As war approached, U.S. intelligence analysts were questioning almost every major piece of WMD intelligence.[2] The CIA chief weapons inspector, David Kay, said:

> "Anything that showed Iraq didn't have weapons of mass destruction had a much higher gate to pass because if it were true, all U.S. policy towards Iraq would have fallen asunder."[3]

In addition to the pressure on CIA analysts to go along, top policymakers sought, and selectively used, raw intelligence data to support their case. As Seymour Hersh reported in *The New Yorker,* this raw data was not exposed to the vigorous scrutiny traditionally followed in the intelligence community. (Bypassing this scrutiny is known as "stovepiping.") The raw data included some furnished by Iraqi defectors and exile groups, who were actively promoting an American invasion of Iraq. Questionable intelligence from these various sources found a receptive audience among Defense Department policymakers and in the Vice-President's office.

Senator Bill Nelson later made public what had transpired in a secret Senate briefing before the war. In this secret briefing, Vice-President Cheney and the CIA Director told Senators that Saddam could deliver biological and chemical weapons (notably anthrax) to our cities along the eastern seaboard— using aerial pilotless vehicles. The Senate had already dealt with a terrible anthrax scare after 9/11 and was in mortal fear of another. Before the invasion, however, our own Air Force and UN inspectors on the ground in Iraq had already determined that the vehicles were probably designed for reconnaissance missions.[4]

Over 100 articles have challenged misleading Administration statements leading up to the war. None of the reasons cited in the congressional authorization for war have proven to be true. None of the 20-odd claims in Secretary Powell's UN presentation have been borne out.[5]

Powell's UN presentation depended on artist conceptions and simulation of the threat. To increase the impact, he held a simulated vial of anthrax in his hand for the world to see. Compare that presentation with the one President Kennedy made during the Cuban missile crisis, when he showed the world photos of actual missiles pointed at the United States. The difference between the two presidents is simple; despite absolute proof, President Kennedy wanted to avoid war whereas President Bush wanted to make war.

Following public outcry over the non-existent WMDs, President Bush spent tens of millions in dollars and manpower trying to unearth the weapons in Iraq. (He also said Saddam wouldn't let the inspectors in, so we had to invade!) Congressional and public dissatisfaction continued and the President finally appointed a commission to investigate prewar intelligence. The Commission Report contained the following major qualification:

> "There is a separate issue of how policymakers used intelligence they were given and how they reflected it in their presentations to Congress and the public. That issue is not within our charter and we therefore did not consider it nor did we express a view on it."

The Commission found that (1) CIA intelligence was wrong, (2) doubts about the intelligence existed within the CIA and other agencies, but they were dismissed, and (3) intelligence analysts worked in a climate of "impending war" that did not encourage skepticism. For example:

- Analysts were forced to complete their work within a three-week time frame.

- Intense policymaker interest contributed to willingness to accept dubious claims and an unwillingness to reject them (worst-case approach).

- The climate shifted the burden of proof from proving that illegal weapons existed to proving that they did not exist.

- Neither analysts nor *users* were open to being told that evidence supporting the assumptions was uncertain or unreliable.

- Analysts thought war was inevitable before they finished their work.[6]

In an explosive and informative documentary, former experts from the CIA, Pentagon and Foreign Service explain how the White House pressured the CIA to conform to the

Administration's desires and misled the nation into war (www.truthuncovered.com). These experts took apart, piece by piece, Secretary Powell's masterful presentation before the UN. They also said CIA intelligence was circumstantial and inferential...and always with qualifications. They said there was intervention into the operations of the CIA, especially by the Vice-President's office. They said it was unethical and immoral for the Administration to constantly connect Iraq to 9/11 and to a "Mushroom Cloud" nuclear program, when there was no *real* evidence of either.

An Army War College report concluded:

- Saddam was deterred and did not present a threat.

- Taking him down was a distraction from the war on terror.

- The anti-terror campaign is unfocused and threatens to dissipate U.S. military resources.

- The U.S. Army is "near the breaking point."[7]

Options to Avoid War

Common sense and diplomacy could have (1) resolved the war hysteria and uncertainty surrounding Iraq's WMD's and (2) developed a consensus within the world community to force regime change and permit free elections.

The first step would have been easy. There were boots on the ground in Iraq—impartial, professional weapons inspectors from around the world. Before the invasion, these inspectors had found no evidence of:

(1) A nuclear program.

(2) Biological weapons being made underground or in mobile labs.

(3) Pilotless planes with a capability to disperse anthrax in the air above U.S. cities.[8]

The inspectors were getting cooperation from Iraq and, despite several tip-offs from American and British intelligence, had found no evidence that Iraq was concealing WMDs. The inspectors wanted more time, but Bush went to war. If the Bush administration did not want to rely solely on international inspectors, all they had to do was send U.S.

experts to participate with them. Secretary Rumsfeld claimed he, in fact, knew the exact location in Iraq of two WMD sites, and Secretary Powell made a number of specific claims at the UN. Any or all of that information could have been checked out before the war by the international inspectors in Iraq—with or without U.S. participation.

It was common knowledge that the CIA did not have a good network of sources in Iraq. The source on mobile biological weapons was a suspected fabricator who was considered mentally unstable. CIA officials say they tried to alert the CIA Director to this situation.[9] In the final analysis, why would any reasonable person rely on CIA assessments and questionable sources when the actual facts were readily available in Iraq?

The next step would have been more difficult to achieve—to diplomatically convince the UN and a coalition of countries to replace the Saddam regime and hold free elections. The U.S. case could have been built on Saddam's aggressive wars in the region, exacerbation of the Israeli/Palestinian conflict by Saddam's rewards to suicide bombers, and his cruel and inhuman treatment of his own people. With Saddam's departure, the UN could administer free elections with the full participation of all three ethnic groups.

To influence world opinion, the U.S. could have showcased an Iraqi democracy as a regional and international benefit. The Bush administration now plans to spend several million dollars in Iran to promote democracy. The same thing could have been done in Iraq.

As for Saddam's removal, he and his chief lieutenants could have elected to move to another country of their choosing, or be captured or killed. Capture would have meant prosecution by an international court for crimes against humanity as The Hague is now doing with people from the Balkan countries. If Saddam's removal required military action, it would have had to be just temporary—with no military occupation or plans to establish military bases.

For this type of peaceful resolution, the Bush administration would have had to alter the far right's fixation on war and, instead, work hand in hand with the international community. Unfortunately, the far right didn't want to take the high road, and many have died or suffered as a result.

An Iraqi woman in Baghdad, who has drawn worldwide respect for her reporting on the personal hardships and daily lives of Iraqis, had this to say about democracy:

> "Democracy has to come from within and it has to be a request of the people—not of expatriates who have alliances with the CIA and British intelligence. People have to want something enough to rise up and change it. They have to be ready for democracy and willing to accept its

responsibility. The U.S. could have promoted democracy in Iraq peacefully, but then they wouldn't have permanent bases in the country, would they?"[10]

Retroactively Justifying Flawed Judgement

Once the major claims of WMDs made in the build-up to war were discredited, the Bush administration put out various "after the fact" reasons for going to war. The following paragraphs identify these reasons and why they are just as invalid as the one on WMDs.

1   *Saddam eventually would have converted facilities from civilian to weapons production, reconstituted his former programs, and passed weapons on to al-Qaeda terrorists.*

There are three problems with this scenario:

First, the President got America's support on the grounds that Iraq was concealing lethal weapons and was an immediate threat to the United States and the region. Clearly, that support would not have been given had the President's case for war been based on assumptions of some remote threat in the future. It is extremely doubtful that such a war authorization would ever have been submitted.

Second, possible conversion of civilian facilities to weapon use is not sufficient reason to justify war. In fact, war could be started on this basis most anywhere in the world, and at any time.

Third, Iraq never before terrorized the United States and was not *then* a terrorist state. Dr. Kay's huge inspection team in Iraq found no evidence of any transfer of illegal weapons to terrorists. CIA analysts were ordered, repeatedly, to redo intelligence assessments to show an Iraqi connection with al-Qaeda, but refused to alter their conclusion.[11] The 9/11 Commission confirmed the CIA analysis.

2 *Iraq is now the central front for the war on terrorism.*

Fighting Iraq had little to do with terrorism until we made it so, by invading a Muslim nation based on false pretenses. There were rumors of an al-Qaeda training camp in the Kurdish north, but that part of Iraq was not under Saddam's control.

3 *If we don't fight the terrorists in Iraq now, we will have to fight them one day in the streets of American cities.*

This is foolish conjecture. There was no problem with terrorists in Iraq until we invaded that country. How do we know that the terrorists there now entertained any thoughts of coming to America? It is far more likely that an unprovoked invasion of a Muslim country has inspired resistance by Iraqi citizens and others who resent our military presence.

4   *Saddam treated his people brutally.*

The Administration has constantly referred to major incidents of brutality that took place many years ago. These incidents were well known to earlier administrations, but Saddam was treated as a valuable ally until the Gulf War. Saddam's atrocities are entirely unrelated to the war on terrorism. These atrocities should have been taken to an international court as crimes against humanity—not used, retroactively, as a pretext for war.

5   *The war was justified "because we removed a regime that did have these weapons and gave us no reason to believe they had eliminated them."*

"Did" is the operative word. In order to avoid a preemptive war, does a country have to prove a negative? Poor Iraqi book-keeping (documenting weapon destruction) does not excuse the war. International weapons experts on the ground were discovering the truth.

6   *The world is a safer/better place without Saddam.*

Actually, Saddam had been defanged. Containing him had

worked. His regime was slowly crumbling under UN sanctions. Both Secretary of State Powell and National Security Advisor Rice said publicly in 2001 that *Saddam posed no threat.*

7   *Congress and countries around the world also believed Saddam had WMD's.*

Politicians and people in the media have used this same excuse. As will be explained in the next sections of this chapter, Congress and the media simply did not do their job. The fact is, they and other countries unwisely relied too much on U.S. intelligence and repetitive statements of the President, Vice-President and Secretary of Defense.

Very early, a year before the invasion, Tony Blair of England committed to support Bush on the war. Later, Blair got information that the intelligence was "thin," but ignored it. (*The Guardian*, John Ware, March, 26, 2005.)

Smaller countries just do not have the big budget, extensive military intelligence apparatus that we do. But, whatever other countries believed, most of them had enough sense to hold out for the facts before agreeing to sign on to a preemptive war. These facts were readily available from ongoing international inspections, which at that time had not discovered a single illegal weapon. Since Bush was dragging the American people into war against the advice of much of the world community, it was his responsibility to get the facts straight and be sure of his position.

8   *We need to spread democracy throughout the Mideast.*

This is the Administration's latest justification for the war. However, the President never told us that planting seeds of democracy would risk many thousands of American lives or cost hundreds of billions of dollars, with no assurance that this costly experiment would work. As a recent Muslim Nobel prize winner said, "democracy is a historical process and cannot be imposed militarily from the outside."[12] The CIA, State Department, and an international consulting firm all warned the Administration about the difficulties of trying to build democracy "on the ashes of Saddam's regime."[13]

Confronted with daily attacks and loss of life, Iraq is now on a long and difficult road to a new government. Much will depend on what kind of Iraqi constitution is agreed to and on whether truly free elections will follow the new constitution. Regardless of the outcome, the election:

> "...does not change the circumstances under which we stumbled to war, does not change the pattern of misstatement, overstatement and will-ful self-deception that has thus far cost nearly

1500 American lives and an untold number of Iraqi lives. Nor does it change the fact that this was the wrong war at the wrong time because it did not serve the most vital issue of *national interest. It did not make us safer from terrorism.*"

—Leonard Pitts Jr., *New York Times*, February 5, 2005

Congress Issues a Blank Check

Against the background of fear and uncertainty, the President received a blank check from an intimidated Congress.

When the President decided prematurely to go to war in Iraq, Congress relied on the same intelligence that he, presumably, used. Under our Constitution, Congress is supposed to be an equal branch and act as one of the checks and balances on the Executive Branch.

Congress did not ask the tough questions, examine evidence, or enter into a serious debate. It did not seek independent information or even ask for actual data from the international inspectors.

Most in Congress fell into lockstep with the President without calling in outside experts to get both sides of the story. Members relied on Administration witnesses and top level officials. In effect, Congress ceded its constitutional war-making power to the President. Congress abandoned the all-important system of checks and balances that our founding fathers had so carefully built into our democracy.

The type of authorization Congress should have given the President is illustrated below. It was sent by a WWII Vet (one of the authors) to representatives in Congress before they authorized the use of force.

Authorizing Use Of Force

Prove whether useable WMDs actually exist in Iraq and pose a threat.

If so, disarm and remove Saddam with International and Regional support.

Cite "Kennedy" model for maximum diplomacy and minimum loss of life on both sides.

Make dismantling al-Qaeda the first priority. Al-Qaeda, not Saddam, brutally attacked us and continues to threaten us.

Can you pass this test—would you support Bush's war if Iraq was not a 5th rate power, or if members of your own family were going to be on the firing line?

In the congressional investigation that followed, the Republican Chairman refused to pursue how the Administration influenced, used, or presented intelligence to Congress and the American people. He said, however, he would do that part of the investigation after the 2004 presidential election. Since then, the chairman has quietly abandoned the investigation.

A Subservient Media

The media is our watchdog. It is the only way the public can find out more than the government chooses to tell us. As our major source of information, the media is the lifeblood of our democracy.

Instead of doing an impartial investigation, the media marched to the drumbeat of the Administration and sent its own people to join military units to report from there. They did not ask the really tough questions or examine evidence beforehand. For example, if banned weapons of the magnitude claimed by the President actually existed, where was the proof of just a few—or even one? Or, even more obvious, why doesn't the Administration use the international inspectors on the ground in Iraq to verify U.S. intelligence? As mentioned, Rumsfeld told reporters publicly that he actually knew of two specific WMD locations. Why didn't reporters ask him if he had confirmed his information with the international inspectors?

The media's tendency was to rely on high-level sources sympathetic to the Administration and on Iraqi defectors and exile groups, instead of doing their own work independently. The coverage of many newspapers was highly deferential to the White House. There were some notable exceptions, such as the *Knight Ridder* newspapers, but they did not receive national attention.[14]

The *New York Times* periodically reported that the threat from Iraq's weapons programs was real and ominous. In May 2004 and again in July 2004, the *Times* published (to its credit) an apology to its readers (1) for running numerous stories containing misinformation and (2) for not challenging the President's assumptions. The *Times* Ombudsman said:

- The *Times* reporting relied on exiles and anonymous Administration sources.

- The *Times* was used to further a cunning campaign to promote WMD stories.

- When these stories broke apart, *Times'* readers never found out why or who the mistaken sources were.[15]

The *Washington Post* ran a major editorial in support of the war. Its editorial assumed facts not in evidence. As Bob Woodward pointed out in his book on the war, his own newspaper downplayed contrary evidence from its reporters by putting their articles on back pages. An investigative report by Howard Kurtz confirms the mistakes of his newspaper. However, the *Washington Post* has not apologized to its readers for having misled them.

Some important observations are contained in a publication entitled *News Incorporated: Corporate Media Ownership and Its Threat to Democracy*:

- Whoever controls the information controls the nation.

- We, the citizens, own the airways but have lost both them and over 80% of independent newspapers to corporate divisions of a few large conglomerate companies, who are concerned more with profit and their political affiliation than with the need to keep the public well informed.

- Federal policies that govern media ownership let this handful of corporate giants swallow up independents and control the media industry.

- Americans receive a censored version of reality, and the watchdog of democracy—the press—has become a docile instrument of government authority and big money. Sensationalism and celebrity gossip have replaced quality journalism.[16]

Nazi Germany's propagandist, Josef Goebbels, said, "Think of the press as a great keyboard on which the government can play." We should all think long and hard about that statement.

Two Possible Exit Strategies

The President insisted on an unnecessary war in Iraq and stubbornly refuses to change his course. As a result, our military has been suffering increasing loss of life and injuries—practically every day. Injuries are approaching 13,000—including permanent disabilities such as blindness, loss of limbs, and mental health problems. Although records are not kept, estimates of Iraqi loss of life and injury exceed 100,000. Cooperation with U.S. occupiers is a death warrant. Undernourished children, rampant disease, and a crippled health system are threatening to do even more damage to Iraqi civilians. After two years of occupation, there are still serious problems involving security, water sewage, electricity, and fuel. The unemployment rate is 50%.[17]

A new major study, by the CIA's National Intelligence Council, reports that Iraq has become a training, recruiting, and breeding ground for a new generation of Islamic terrorists.[18] U.S. plans for military bases in Iraq will further inflame the Muslim world and increase terrorism.

Many in the military believe the war is a disaster. Never have there been such bad feelings between the military and civilian leadership in the Pentagon. It is unreasonable to expect our military to continue absorbing losses for a war we didn't have to fight. Before the war we thumbed our nose at most of the rest of the world. We can hardly expect them to come to our rescue—putting their lives on the line for miscalculations of the Bush administration. More than a third of the countries have dropped out of the U.S.-led coalition. The President has submitted, as part of his new war supplemental, $400 million to reward (coax) others to remain.[19]

Our continued presence in Iraq is causing most, if not all, of the resistance and acts of terror. From the Iraqi's perspective, we are the foreigners who invaded their country, and who are stealing their oil and killing many thousands of civilians—including women and children. When our military occupation ends, so will the insurgency. The insurgents and outside terrorists will no longer have a mission. Several polls conducted by both American and Iraqi media show that most Iraqis want American troops to leave soon. They believe our presence "does not provide security for the average Iraqi, and it never has." More than half the American people surveyed think the Iraqi war "was not worth fighting."

The Iraqi people should decide their own destiny. An American president would be widely acclaimed here and around the world if he would adopt a reasonable exit strategy adaptable to changing circumstances on the ground. Here are two possibilities:

Strategy # 1—Start with partial withdrawal

An article urges a new direction with a five-step program to begin withdrawal of our troops. (Erik Leaver, "A New Course in Iraq" *Foreign Policy in Focus*, December 10, 2004.) It concludes the following:

- "The current U.S. approach in Iraq is too costly in human and financial terms to Americans at home, our troops abroad, and to the very people this war was supposed to liberate."

- "…the U.S. needs to accept the fact that continued military occupation by the U.S. will only cause more casualties, foster division in the country, and keep reconstruction from advancing."

- "More Iraqi security force recruits and Iraqi police officers have been killed than Americans. Iraqi security forces can't succeed as long as the U.S. is leading a war on the ground."

The Five Steps Set Forth in the Article to Exit Iraq are:

1   Declare an immediate cease-fire and reduce the number of troops. Total withdrawal would depend on strengthened Iraqi security forces and assistance from Muslim countries.

2   Declare no intention to maintain a permanent or long-term military presence or bases in Iraq.

3   Accelerate reconstruction giving Iraqis more control over funding; increase Iraqi jobs and projects targeted to the country's needs.

4   The prospects of *fully participatory* elections by *all* ethnic groups any time soon are dim. Focus on local government at the grass roots.

5   Congress should shape U.S. policy by tying war supplementals to such points as the ones above.

Strategy # 2—Start with immediate withdrawal to the borders

1   Totally withdraw our military, but maintain about 60,000 along the borders—with a quick response capability—until a *constitutional* government is installed.

2   Allow any country willing and able to fully participate in reconstruction. Accelerate reconstruction, but only if Iraqi and other Muslim security forces maintain safe conditions. Failure to do this would automatically terminate U.S. participation.

These two strategies are ways to extricate ourselves from an impossible situation that the President has led us into. Either will give the Iraqi people a decent chance to create their own version of democracy as well as incentives to secure their country.

Needed—Broader Strategy on Terror

The Bush administration response to terror has been side-tracked with a war in Iraq which has spread our military too thin. Further, the response is too limited in scope to solve a global problem and does not address the root causes of terrorism.

An Asian-Pacific conference on security concluded that the world is losing the war on terror because the United States has expanded the sea of hatred and deep-seated rage in the Muslim world. The conference also deduced that the use of force alone cannot eliminate terrorist threats.[20]

In a *New York Times* article, top terrorism expert Richard Clarke contends that the United States is headed in the wrong direction. He claims that trying to impose real democracy on an Arab nation at the end of an American bayonet is "dead on arrival." To eliminate terrorism, he says, we must have the support of the moderate Muslim community.

The President's idea that the U.S. can deal with each and every country that supports or harbors terrorists is foolish bravado and impossible to achieve. Eliminating worldwide terrorism is a shared responsibility that requires leadership and cooperation from all heads of state. A global problem needs a global solution. This demands a more comprehensive and aggressive worldwide strategy.

The Essential Elements (Costing a Fraction of War) are:

- Mandate, through the United Nations, each nation's responsibility to remove terrorist activities in their own country and help others do the same.

- Outlaw bomb-making nuclear material, inspect all countries that might give such material to terrorists, and enforce severe penalties for violations. The UN is moving in this direction.

- Withdraw U.S. forces from Muslim countries and participate in peacekeeping through the UN and NATO.

- Sponsor a UN commission to identify the root causes of terrorism and determine remedies.

- Put as much U.S. power and prestige behind building a Palestinian state as we have done in building Israel.

- Make energy independence one of America's highest priorities. Terrorists may adopt the strategy of disrupting major sources of oil (in Saudi Arabia for example), as they are now doing in Iraq.

- Encourage religious spokespeople around the world to stress the many similarities between the Christian, Jewish and Muslim faiths.

The international community must declare war on terror worldwide and use the military power and intelligence of every country to win that war. Each country should operate from a mandate to dismantle terrorism and assist other countries in need of help. Any country not relentlessly pursuing terrorists or continuing to support them should receive sanctions, be suspended from the UN, and be subject to military action. Periodically, the UN should hold head-of-state meetings and deal forcefully with those countries not making progress. Let's really get serious.

The United States helped give birth to the UN to maintain peace in the world, and its headquarters are in our country. Instead of demeaning and undermining it as the far right has consistently done, we should support that body and help reform it to work effectively for all.

In parallel with this action, the United States should sponsor an international commission to identify fundamental changes that would reverse the root causes of organized violent behavior in the world. People everywhere need hope that one day we will turn to more peaceful ways, without a fortress mentality.

The Bottom Line

As 2002 midterm elections approached, President Bush intimidated Congress into passing open-ended authority, allowing him to use force in Iraq. He then manipulated our nation into an unprovoked and costly conflict. This conflict has created a "terrorist jungle" in a country that posed no threat.

By staging a unilateral, preemptive war based on poor information, the Administration has opened Pandora's Box. We have set a horrible precedent, and America's good name is under attack. It will take at least a decade to repair America's credibility and rebuild trust in our Government.

The diplomatic and peaceful solution was to explore all avenues and go to war only as a last resort. By promoting democracy and working with the international community on regime change, Iraq could have been persuaded to embrace a more democratic form of government.

Bush is still ducking responsibility for the crisis his Administration created. Urged on by the far right, he bears the responsibility for his words, decisions, and the people he has appointed. The buck stops at his desk.

Bush's tone, in his public utterances, is that his noble objective of advancing freedom will somehow absolve him of the many mistakes he made during the lead up to war and occupation. History will not be so kind.

The reader should wonder whether terrorist attacks around the world would have escalated if the United States had focused on al-Qaeda, instead of diverting our military power to Iraq.

Congress should not fund supplementals for the war in Iraq without setting specific conditions that the President must meet.

The public must become better informed and wake up to the failures of Congress and the media in dealing with the Executive Branch's misuse of power. We need to send better representatives to Congress, ones who are willing and able to carry out their obligations under our Constitution.

As Bill Moyers pointed out at a major media conference in May 2005, "The media is being corrupted by big business and government power." Public hearings are needed to inquire into the conduct of the media's role in our democracy. Looming issues include real independence from those reported on, excessive concentration of ownership, and conflict of interest between that ownership and the people's right to know.

A far-reaching and independent investigation is still needed into the legality of the war and how the Bush administration influenced, used, and presented intelligence to Congress and the American people.

Endnotes

1   "Panel: U.S. Ignored Work of UN Arms Inspectors" Dafna Linzer, *Washington Post*, April 3, 2005. Three sources contributed to Ms. Linzer's article: (1) sources in the *Commission Report* such as page 59 and footnotes 72 and 299, (2) research of inspection reports on the UN website (Briefings of UNMOVIC and IAEA to the UN on March 7, 2003), and (3) her 6-month stay in Iraq with the WMD survey group; "Now They Tell Us" *The New York Review of Books*, February 26, 2004, pp. 10-18; "Prewar Findings Worried Analysts" Walter Pincus, *Washington Post*, May 22, 2005.

2   "CIA shapes intelligence data to meet administration policy goals" *Washington Post*, June 12, 2003; "Ex-Spies: CIA Workers Outraged" *CBS news.com*, July 19, 2003; "Prewar Findings Worried Analysts" Walter Pincus, *Washington Post*, May 22, 2005.

3   "Kay Report/No WMD, No Case for War" *Star Tribune*, Oct. 4, 2003; Dr. Kay's testimony and public statements, January/February 2004.

4   "Senators were told Iraqi weapons could hit U.S." *Florida Today.com*, December 15, 2003; "Prewar Findings Worried Analysts" Walter Pincus, *Washington Post*, May 22, 2005.

5 "Not Enough Swords to Go Around" Richard Cohen, *Washington Post*, July 27, 2003.

6 "The Commission on the Intelligence Capabilities of the United States Regarding Weapons of Mass Destruction" *Biological Warfare Findings 3 and 4*, Conclusions 12, 24, and 26, March 31, 2005; "A Final Verdict on Prewar Intelligence Is Still Elusive" Todd Purdum, *New York Times*, April 1, 2005.

7 "Study Published by Army Criticize War on Terror's Scope" *Washington Post*, January 12, 2004.

8 "Panel: U.S. Ignored Work of UN Arms Inspectors," Dafna Linzer, *Washington Post*, April 3, 2005. Three sources contributed to Ms. Linzer article: (1) sources in the *Commission Report* such as page 59 and footnotes 72 and 299, (2) research of inspection reports on the UN website (Briefings of UNMOVIC and IAEA to the UN on March 7, 2003) and (3) her 6-month stay in Iraq with the WMD survey group; Also see "Now They Tell Us" *The New York Review of Books*, February 26, 2004, pp. 10-18; "Prewar Findings Worried Analysts" Walter Pincus, *Washington Post*, May 22, 2005.

9 "The Commission on the Intelligence Capabilities of the United States Regarding Weapons of Mass Destruction" *Biological Warfare Finding 4*, March 31, 2005.

10 *Buzzflash* interview with a Baghdad blogger, April 15, 2005.

11 "Questions Grow Over Iraq Links to al-Qaeda" Peter Canellos and Bryon Bender, *Boston Globe*, August 3, 2003; "CIA Felt Pressure to Alter Iraq Data, Author Says" *Common Dreams New Center*, July 1, 2004; "CIA Finds No Evidence Hussein Sought to Arm Terrorists" *Washington Post*, November 16, 2003.

12 "Nobel winner says U.S. cannot impose democracy" *Reuters*, June 3, 2004.

13 "Democracy Might Be Impossible, U.S. Was Told" *Boston Globe*, August 14, 2003.

14 "Where Was the Media?" *Center for American Progress Report*, February 11, 2004; "Now They Tell Us" *The New York Review of Books,* February 26, 2004.

15 "*New York Times* ombudsman prints withering critique of Iraq coverage" *U.S. National*, May 30, 2004.

16 Cohen, Elliot, *News Incorporated: Corporate Media Ownership And Its Threat To Democracy*, Prometheus Books, 2005; "Who Owns the Media" *Free Press*, January 2, 2005.

17 "A New Course in Iraq" *Foreign Policy In Focus*, December 10, 2004.

18 "Report Says Iraq Is New Terrorist Training Ground" *Washington Post*, January 13, 2005.

19 "Bush asks millions as reward for allies" *Associated Press*, February 10, 2005.

20 "Report: al-Qaeda Ranks Swelling Worldwide" *Nation/World News,* May 26, 2004; "Al-Qaeda winning: Asian analysts" *The Age*, May 31, 2004.

Other Sources

"A State Department report disputes Bush's claim that ousting Hussein will spur reforms in the Mideast" *Los Angeles Times*, March 14, 2003

"Democracy Domino Theory Not Credible" Greg Miller, *Los Angeles Times*, March 14, 2003.

"A reckless path" *The Washington Times*, March 20, 2003.

"Hunt for Iraqi Arms Erodes Assumptions" *Washington Post*, April 22, 2003.

"Assessing the Weapons Search" *New York Times*, April 26, 2003.

"Revealed: How the road to war was paved with lies" *Independent.co.uk*, April 27, 2003.

"The Most Dangerous President Ever" *The American Prospect*, May 1, 2003.

"Neoconservative clout seen in U.S. policy" *Milwaukee Journal Sentinel*, May 10, 2003.

"Karl Rove's Campaign Strategy: It's the Terror" *New York Times*, May 10, 2003.

"Frustrated, U.S. Arms Team to Leave Iraq" *Washington Post*, May 11, 2003.

"Bush Officials Change Tune on Iraqi Weapons" *Reuters*, May 14, 2003.

"WMD just a convenient excuse for war, admits Wolfowitz" *Independent.co.uk*, May 30, 2003.

"Iraq repercussions trouble top advisors" *The Mercury News*, May 31, 2003.

"Truth and consequences" *US NEWS.com*, June 3, 2003.

John Dean articles dissecting the President's State of the Union speech, *Find Law's Legal Commentary*, June 6 and July 18, 2003.

Ed Asner and Burt Hall

"Ex-Official: Evidence Distorted for War" *Associated Press*, June 8, 2003.

"Bush's deception on Iraqi intelligence" *The Boston Globe*, June 8, 2003

"Reasons to Deceive" *Reuters*, June 18, 2003.

"CIA Officer: Bush Ignored Warnings" *Knight Ridder*, June 13, 2003.

"10 Appalling Lies We Were Told About Iraq" *AlterNet.org*, June 27, 2003.

"White House lied about Saddam threat" *Guardian Unlimited*, July 11, 2003.

"20 Lies about the War" *Independent.co.uk*, July 13, 2003.

"Pattern of Corruption" Paul Krugman, *New York Times*, July 15, 2003.

"Ten Questions for Cheney" *TomPaine.com*, July 22, 2003;

Full-page ads in 3 major newspapers challenging the honesty of the Bush administration (e.g. *New York Times*, July 27, 2003).

"The Bush Administration's Top 40 lies About War and Terrorism" *CityPages.com*, July 30, 2003.

"Scientists Still Deny Iraqi Arms Programs" *Washington Post*, July 31, 2003.

"Prewar statements by Cheney under scrutiny" *Chicago Tribune*, August 6, 2003.

"Depiction of Threat Outgrew Supporting Evidence" Barton Gellman and Walter Pincus, *Washington Post*, August 10, 2003.

"U.S. Justification for War: How it Stacks Up Now" *Associated Press*, *Seattle Times*, August 10, 2003.

"Today we face another Watergate" *Newsday.com.*, August 11, 2003.

"The Bush Deceit" Peter Zimmerman, *Washington Post.com* August 14, 2003.

"A Price Too High" *New York Times*, August 21, 2003.

"AP Staffer Fact-Checks Powell's UN Speech....Key Claims Didn't Hold Up" *Editor & Publisher*, September 9, 2003.

"Will Press Roll Over Again on New WMD report?" *Editor & Publisher*, September 10, 2003.

Time Magazine Iraqi survey, October 6, 2003.

"Deception Down Under" *Tom Paine Common Sense*, October 14, 2003.

"Ex-Aide: Powell Misled Americans" *CBSNEWS.com*, October 15, 2003.

"Sen. Hagel Says Congress Deferred Too Much to Bush" *Washington Post*, October 21, 2003.

"The Stovepipe" Seymour Hersh, *New Yorker*, October 27, 2003.

"No president has lied so badly and so often and so demonstrably" *Independent.co.uk*, November 19, 2003.

"War critics astonished as U.S. hawk admits invasion was illegal" *Guardian Unlimited*, November 26, 2003.

"Medical evacuations from Iraq near 11,000" *United Press International*, December 19, 2003.

"The Burden of Truth" *Sojourners*, December 20, 2003.

"Iraq's Arsenal Was Only On Paper" *Washington Post*, January 7, 2004.

"White House Distorted Iraq Threat" *Financial Times*, January 10, 2004.

"New WMD Report Slams Bush White House" *AlterNet.org*, January 13, 2004.

"Bush, Aides Ignored CIA Caveats on Iraq" *Washington Post*, February 7, 2004.

"Needed: A New and Bolder Strategy for the War on Terror" Ed Asner and Burt Hall, *Humanist*, July/August 2004.

"The Use of Intelligence" *Boston Globe*, February 6, 2004.

"Meet the Facts" *Center for American Progress Report*, February 9, 2004.

Laurence Silberman: The Right Man or the Right's Man, Press Release, *People For The American Way*, February 13, 2004.

"British spy wrecked peace move" *Guardian Unlimited*, February 15, 2004.

"10% at Hospital Had Mental Problems" *Military.com*, February 19, 2004.

"Bush Wanted War in 2002" *Guardian Unlimited*, February 24, 2002.

"Hans Blix Says Iraq War Was Unfounded" *Guardian Unlimited*, February 24, 2004.

"The Hollow Army" James Fallows, *The Atlantic*, March 2004.

"Blix states Iraq war was illegal" *Nettanisen*, March 5, 2004.

Woodward, Bob, *Plan of Attack*, Simon & Schuster, 2004.

"U.S. admits the war for hearts and minds in Iraq is now lost" *Sunday Herald*, December 5, 2004. [Pentagon report reveals catalogue of failures]

"CIA Agent Says Bosses Ordered Him to Falsify WMD Reports" *Democracy Now*, December 16, 2004.

"Analysis: Only U.S. can damage self majorly despite bin Laden" *Associated Press*, December 18, 2004. [bin Laden bleeding superpowers]

"The Butcher's Bill" [A look at the future of the war in Iraq], Jack Beatty, *Atlantic Unbound*, December 26, 2004.

"An army's morale on the downswing" William Pfaff, *International Herald Tribune*, December 29, 2004.

"Lauria Garret of *Newsday* Rips *Tribune Co.* Greed in Exit Memo" *Editor & Publisher*, March 1, 2005.

"Why Iraq Withdrawal Makes Sense" Norman Solomon, *Common Dreams News Center*, March 17, 2005.

"The coalition of the wilting" *Chicago Tribune*, March 21, 2005.

"M16, Jack Straw, defense staff: Blair ignored them all, John Ware" *Guardian Unlimited*, March 26, 2005.

"WMD Commission Stonewalls" *The Nation*, April 1, 2005.

"Who Forged the Niger Documents?" Ian Masters, *AlterNet.org*, April 7, 2005

"Bush asked to explain UK war memo" *CNN.com*, May 12, 2005.

"Prewar Findings Worried Analysts" Walter Pincus, *Washington Post*, May 22, 2005.

"Memo: Bush manipulated Iraq intel" *Knight Ridder* Newspaper, May 9, 2005.

"The Secret Way to War" Mark Donner, *The New York Review of Books*, June 9, 2005.

Chapter Five

Satire—How Far Right Won Second Term

"Like greed, aggression is good. Aggression has
marked the upward surge of mankind. Aggression
breeds patriotism, and patriotism curbs dissent.
Aggression has made Democrats cower, the press
purr and the world quake. Aggression—you mark
my words—will not only save humanity, but it will
soon color all the states Republican red."

—Maureen Dowd, *New York Times*, May 4, 2003

This chapter is a satire—based, though, on real events. It gives
you some insight into how President Bush and his far-right advisors *might* have responded to the warnings leading up to 9/11,
how they convinced themselves that it was a good idea to go to
war in Iraq, and how they personally benefited from the war.

Saddam had not bothered the outside world since Father Bush put him in a box. Most of his weapons had been destroyed during UN inspections. In 2001, Iraq was not an issue; both Secretary Powell and National Security Advisor Rice said publicly that *Iraq posed no threat*. Many have wondered how and why such an imminent threat suddenly appeared on our doorsteps. The following is based on actual facts, but speculates on what Bush might have said to himself and aides as events unfolded.

Well, I made up my mind early that I wasn't going to suffer my dad's fate—a one-term presidency. Things didn't go smoothly, though. I'll tell you what happened; then tell me what you would have done.

Warnings Don't Scare Us

It all started when Clinton and his top aides told us al-Qaeda would be our number one problem and gave us a plan to put their network out of business. Clinton was so upset with these guys, he actually had authorized the CIA to assassinate their leader, Osama bin Laden.

Well, we sure weren't going to let the Democrats set our priorities. Besides, there were other threats to worry about, like North Korea, Iran, and Iraq, and we already had a full plate. For example, I had to get those big tax cuts through to save the economy and help our big contributors. And, these guys were demanding that we reverse some of Clinton's policies, particularly those in the environmental field.

The missile shield was important, too. Congress tried to shift some of my missile shield money to antiterrorism but Rummy told them to go jump in the lake. He even threatened a veto—and I would have done it too! I like playing hardball with those goons in Congress.

Then, Cheney received a briefing confirming Osama was the guy behind the *U.S.S. Cole* attack. But, there was no big hurry—we would eventually deal with him. Next, some folks from a national security commission came over to the White House to warn us that a catastrophe would soon happen here in the United States. They actually tried to tell us how to reorganize the government—something about a Homeland Security Department! Well, we listened and then politely excused them. We had bigger fish to fry!

As summer approached, our intelligence people were picking up all sorts of alarms of impending attacks on our country, but, as you know by now, our intelligence is, at best, questionable. Besides, the economy was shaky. I didn't want to scare the American people and make things worse.

By early August, warnings of impending attacks had become more intense. So, while on vacation at the ranch, some CIA people came down to give me the latest scoop. They told me Osama wanted to strike the U.S. and mentioned the possibility of airplane hijackings. I love my ranch and had a lot of brush to clear and fish to catch, so I figured these problems could wait a few more weeks until September.

Meanwhile, the FBI requested $50 million for their anti-terrorism program. We rejected that, of course. These guys will say anything to get more money.

Then, to our shock and amazement a bunch of terrorists actually had the gall to blow up the World Trade buildings, and attack the Pentagon. A fourth plane that went down in Pennsylvania probably was headed for me! Although we'd had warnings from many other countries about this, we didn't believe they'd actually do it.

Well, I have to pat myself on the back—I handled the aftermath like a pro. After my aggressive response to the tragedy, I was "lookin' good"—until some do-gooders in Congress tried to create a commission to find out why we were caught so flatfooted. We couldn't let that happen. So, what would you have done? Just what I did, I'm sure—oppose the Commission on the grounds that they would interfere with our national security.

Those 9/11 Families Dare to Challenge My Cover-up

That worked for almost a year. But, it was just my luck that those 9/11 families persisted with this commission idea. I don't mind telling Congress where to get off, which I sometimes do in private, but no president in his right mind would oppose those 9/11 families. I'm sure you would have caved in, too.

Give me some credit, though. I modified the Commission as best I could. In the final deal we got a Republican to chair the Commission and succeeded in limiting their subpoena power. Cheney pulled the strings behind the scenes in Congress. He and others on my staff feared the Commission might send us what amounts to a "pink slip" just when the presidential campaign was heating up. So, here comes the tough part—how could we neutralize the Commission's work?

Well, first we had to set up an obstacle course for the Commission. We insisted that Ashcroft screen all the Commission's requests for information and that agency monitors be present at Commission interviews—like Saddam did when the UN tried to interview his scientists. I'm just as tough as Saddam, and we simply can't have our people talking out of turn with no retribution. As far as full access to all my CIA briefings and national security meetings— "over my cold dead body!"

Rove Says We Must Have a Wartime President

Meanwhile, Rove told me, "It's the terror, not the economy, Stupid!" You'll never know how happy I was to hear that—except I didn't like the way he used the word "Stupid." Anyway, we decided it would be a good idea to promote my image as a warrior president for the upcoming midterm elections.

Since we couldn't find my old friend Osama "dead or alive," we needed another terrorist to zero in on. And my buddies, Cheney, Rummy, and Wolfie insisted our old nemesis, Saddam, would fill the bill. They had long wished for his overthrow anyway and had previously authored papers on the subject. Saddam was in trouble with the UN and had little international standing. We could kill two birds with one stone—get Saddam and capture a "terrorist" for the American people. They'd really love me then. We'd argue too that we couldn't wait—we had to get him before he got us.

Saddam had kicked the UN inspectors out several years ago, so by now we figured he must have amassed quite a few illegal weapons. To make this *really* explosive, we decided to link Saddam to al-Qaeda—after all they probably were in cahoots. Also, Saddam probably had a nuclear capability in the works. Wow! All I'd have to do is mention "mushroom cloud" and the public will insist on preempting the evil one.

Then, Rove gave me this idea—why not build a strong case,

surface it just before midterm elections, and back Congress into a corner? Few would dare oppose me and risk their chances for reelection. A congressional OK would also eliminate any danger of impeachment. After all, my potential impeachers had agreed with me. How do you like my idea, so far? Not bad, huh?

As for the war itself that would be a slam dunk! Several of our states are larger than pathetic, defenseless, little Iraq. It doesn't have air or sea power, or smart bombs like us. Should be a piece of cake! This idea was really beginning to appeal to me. Of all my presidential duties, being Commander in Chief is the one I enjoy most.

The icing on the Saddam cake, of course, would be the distraction from our domestic problems. The wartime situation will silence our critics and, in the upcoming elections, we might even regain full control of Congress.

As you mull this over, you'll have to admit, your President is a lot smarter than most people think. This "simple plan" will distract the public from my pre-9/11 responsibility and domestic problems, and perhaps get us back in the driver's seat in Congress. Talk about "wagging the dog!" I'm sure Robert DeNiro and Dustin Hoffman would be proud of me. Before reading any further, tell me what you think of my plan—you'd have done the same thing, right?

No Illegal Weapons—What Now?

There was just one hitch. The war went really well, except that Saddam fooled me; he didn't use a single unlawful weapon against us and we've found no visible signs of any weaponized chemical or biological agents. Bummer! To make things worse, we've not been able to find a nuclear program or a link to either al-Qaeda or 9/11.

I wonder what happened to all those dangerous chemical and biological agents, and the 30,000 munitions to deliver them, I so confidently spoke about in my State of the Union speech. Darn, I was banking so much on those weapons to justify the war. I thought we were being guided by God's hand; how could we have been so wrong?

Saddam must have hidden them somewhere. I guess I'll have to throw thousands of people into the hunt. If we don't find them, we'll settle for some WMD scientists, buried remnants of earlier programs, and the bad intentions of the evil one.

Of course, it's possible that Iraq destroyed its weapons before the war but that would mean the UN inspections, backed with the threat of military power, were actually working. Say it ain't so! I guess, just between you and me, it's also possible that my daddy's war and many long years of UN sanctions, inspections, and flyovers had transformed Iraq into a minor threat, if a threat at all.

The American people do have a short attention span, so I'm just not going to worry about it. Besides, we can dream up lots of other justifications for the war. I'll put Rove on that—just in case we need them.

The Bottom Line

Wasn't all this worth sparing me my daddy's fate—the agony of defeat at reelection time? Sure, Kennedy accepted responsibility for the Bay of Pigs disaster, but 9/11 was much worse. If I had accepted some responsibility for that, it would have taken a miracle to get reelected. If things really get bad, we can always blame Clinton for 9/11—just like we did for other things that have gone wrong in my Administration.

I think I'll push back my second-term acceptance speech at the Republican National Convention in New York City so I can commemorate the third anniversary of 9/11 with all those heroic firemen. That would mean a campaign built around national security and combating terrorism. This should really work to our advantage. We can have a big celebration right there in Madison Square Garden, near Ground Zero. Then, with a couple hundred million dollars in my campaign coffers, the election is mine—all mine.

Chapter Six

Far Right Continues To Misuse Power In Second Term

The President's second term followed the closest election in history for an incumbent or for a wartime president. This chapter answers such questions as: Will there be significant changes in foreign or domestic policy or for budget priorities? Will the far-right Bush administration continue to misuse power and misgovern our country? Where do we go from here?

The current Administration has been seeking radical change. Their extreme actions have had a profound effect on our fiscal condition, as well as on domestic and foreign policy. In many countries, our President is now unwelcome, distrusted, and largely ignored. He "is more widely and deeply disliked in Europe than any U.S. president in history."[1] With minor exceptions, the President's 2005 Inaugural and State of the Union speeches will keep the country on the same far-right course.

National Security

Our military forces, National Guard, and reserves are currently tied up in Iraq and in other occupations around the world. Recruitment goals are not being met. Not enough personnel are left stateside to fight a war, if we had to. The President's State of the Union address failed to acknowledge this or include any major plan to redirect our forces. The Chairman of the Joint Chiefs, in a special message to Congress, admitted that current wars would make it far more difficult for the U.S. military to respond to "future acts of aggression, launch a preemptive strike, or intervene to prevent a conflict in another part of the world."[2]

Elections in Iraq attracted a large turnout, but that didn't really legitimize the decision to take America to war. Continued U.S. occupation will only lead to further bloodshed for American soldiers and innocent Iraqis. Between July 2004 and March 2005, there were over 15,000 attacks against Coalition Forces. The U.S. presence is a target of opportunity for the insurgents. Moreover, the longer our occupation continues the more it undermines the credibility of the regime in power. The bottom line is that neither our soldiers nor Iraqis will be secure—as long as we remain.

For more than two years, the U.S military has been trying to train Iraqi security forces and has consistently overstated their capability and dedication. In the spring of 2005, the U.S. Government Accountability Office issued a report challenging Pentagon claims on readiness of Iraqi security forces. Among its findings were: (1) training of many Iraqi soldiers and police officers "did not prepare them to fight against well-armed insurgents," (2) there is "questionable loyalty" and "poor leadership," and (3) "the number of absentees is probably in the tens of thousands."[3]

Local military commanders privately told a congressional delegation that Iraq is at least two years away from having a ready military. For a down-to-earth and more shocking assessment, read a report from journalists who accompanied U.S./Iraqi units in the field. ("Building Iraq's Army: Mission Improbable" *Washington Post Foreign Service*, June 10, 2005).

The Iraqi government is unlikely to assume full responsibility for putting down the insurgency of their own people as long as they can use coalition forces as a crutch. To unify *all* political factions in Iraq there must be a firm commitment to remove U.S. troops and military bases. That commitment will provide the incentive for Iraqis to build a strong security force and will lead to the decline, if not ultimate demise, of the insurgency.

The President strongly implied in his second-term Inaugural Address that promoting democracies would eliminate tyranny and reduce the threat of terrorism, but he has not shown a connection between the two. He has never told the public what the root causes of terrorism are, or explained how terrorism would dissipate simply by expanding freedom. Some of the root causes are serious east vs. west policy differences, cultural and religious differences, and objections to U.S. intervention in Muslim countries.

Many American presidents over the past century have encouraged building democracies around the world, as did Wilson and Kennedy. Others were directly involved in expanding freedom, such as Roosevelt and Truman (Germany/Japan), Eisenhower (South Korea), Reagan (eastern European countries), and Clinton (Bosnia/Serbia/Kosovo). None of these past presidents expanded freedom by unilaterally destroying much of a country, killing many of its citizens, and wasting hundreds of billions of dollars.

Today, the rate of terrorist attacks around the world is the highest in 20 years. After stalling for several months, the Administration finally released a report in mid-2005 showing a massive increase in world-wide terrorism—three times over the past year. The President doesn't seem to realize that until root causes are addressed, we'll never make inroads toward eradicating terrorism.

Another huge drain on our defense budget is a Star-Wars-type missile shield program. It is supposed to protect us from long-range missile attacks by countries like North Korea. In mid-2001, that program took priority over terrorism, when the President threatened a veto if Congress shifted missile money to counterterrorism. The Administration ordered the missile system to be deployed by the end of 2004. It has not been deployed and is failing tests.[4] As of spring 2005, no new date for the missile shield deployment has been set, but the President continues to spend huge sums on the program. Meanwhile, not enough attention has been given to the more-likely threat of a short-range, low-flying cruise missile or rocket attack, fired by terrorists from ships off the U.S. coast.[5]

The Administration is planning space weapons that have huge implications. As pointed out in a *New York Times* article of May 18, 2005:

- American space superiority is being sought and the financial, technological, political, and diplomatic hurdles will be enormous.

- Other countries will not accept that space is an American frontier and another arms race will ensue.

- Three years of work and billions of dollars already have been spent on weapons that can operate in space and destroy satellites of other countries.

- This proposed effort is the reason for Bush's withdrawal from the 30-year Anti-Ballistic Missile Treaty, which banned space weapons.

Like the airways, no one has a monopoly on space and everybody owns it. Any U.S. attempt to gain space superiority will cost astronomical amounts. If we try to achieve superiority, it will threaten the larger nuclear states and they are likely to respond with an arms race or a preemptive attack. Similar plans were vetoed by the Clinton White House.

Foreign Policy

Over the years a number of countries have joined the nuclear club, once monopolized by the U.S. and Russia. Under a 1970's worldwide non-proliferation treaty, nations without nuclear weapons pledge not to pursue them, in exchange for a commitment by nuclear states to negotiate toward disarmament. However, other countries believe the nuclear states are moving too slowly. In particular, they are concerned with the Bush administration's decisions to reject a nuclear test ban, build new nuclear weapons, and devaluate treaties and the authority of international law.

Two more countries now want to join the club—North Korea and Iran. The usual rationale for ownership of these weapons is that they will increase the regime's status and deter enemy attack. The Administration could have avoided confrontation with these two countries by using strong positive inducements and a *quid pro quo* approach to solving the problem. Instead, the Bush administration has insulted both regimes to the point that they may resist a diplomatic solution and continue their nuclear programs in self defense. Making the situation worse, our hands are not clean in the nuclear field. It is even conceivable that the Administration does not want the North Korea threat to quickly disappear so that it can justify huge missile defense and space programs.

Nuclear proliferation is the preeminent national security issue of our times. One hundred ninety countries met at the UN in mid 2005 to find ways to strengthen the proliferation treaty. As a *New York Times* editorial pointed out, the conference failed to close gaping holes in the treaty even though control over nuclear technology is "fundamental to our survival." Neither the President nor the Secretary of State found time to attend.

It is impossible to imagine the utter destruction that can result from today's nuclear bombs—even a small one. A leading expert, former Secretary of Defense Robert McNamara, has described in the *Foreign Policy* May/June 2005 issue the incalculable damage that would result from just one of these bombs. He characterizes our nuclear policy and its "hair-trigger" response as immoral, illegal, militarily unnecessary, and dreadfully dangerous. He believes that the U.S. must *lead* the way toward *elimination* of these weapons around the world and should no longer rely on them as a foreign policy tool.[6]

To convince the American people to give him a first term, Bush took the view that America, the only remaining super-power, should exercise restraint and project humility in our relations with other countries—"and this will be the spirit of my administration." Instead, the "spirit" of Bush's administration has been just the opposite. He and his far-right advisors have taken an arrogant, "my way or the highway" posture, acting unilaterally instead of working with the international community on common problems. "The U.S. is now viewed as a brutal, bullying, nation that countenances torture and operates hideous prison camps."[7] In late January 2005, Tom Friedman of the *New York Times* spent 10 days touring four European countries. He found universal dislike and distrust of the President.

"Bush took away our America. I mean, we love America. We are very sad about America. We believe in America and American values, but not in Bush. And, it makes us angry that he distorted our image of the country which is so important to us."[7a]

—Tim Kreutzfeldt, a European

A 2004 Defense Science Board study reported there is world-wide anger and discontent over the ways the U.S. pursues its goals, and these ways have "…played straight into the hands of al-Qaeda." A letter to Secretary Powell (Appendix I) explains why a high-level diplomat resigned his position in the Bush administration. The letter is a wide-ranging and eloquent analysis of how our foreign policy and the war in Iraq have affected our position around the world. The analysis leaves no doubt that we need to restore our standing as a respected world leader.

Fiscal Policy

The Bush administration's economic policies have replaced the large surpluses left by the Clinton administration with a staggering debt for future generations. Our long-term fiscal health is in serious jeopardy, and the President's State of the Union speech did not point to any fundamental change in direction. The President promises, though, to cancel a number of federal programs and eventually reduce the annual deficit in half. We've heard that promise before from this same President.

For example, the President predicts a decline from this year's record $427 billion deficit to $390 billion in 2006. But, if you add the continuing cost of war in Iraq and other omissions from the proposed budget, you'll find we are actually headed for new record deficits.[8]

Things will go from bad to worse. According to an analysis of the new budget figures, the President's successor will have *massive financial commitments that rise dramatically in the year Bush leaves office.* Extensive tax cuts that the President wants to make permanent will contribute to this escalating problem. The next President could be spending his entire four-year term "figuring out how to accommodate the long-range cost of Bush's policies."[9]

Fiscal responsibility became a major issue during the 1992 presidential election. By supporting the global economy, improving the business environment, and raising taxes, President Clinton eventually balanced the budget and started paying down our national debt. Instead of trying to continue that trend, President Bush has exploded the federal deficit and shifted the tax burden from the wealthy to the middle class.

Trade deficits, annual budget deficits, and the national debt have reached all-time highs. Add to this Bush's pending tax cuts, entitlement reforms, and continued presence in Iraq, and you have a fiscal condition out of control. Increasing the debt in times of financial crisis will lead to higher interest rates and runaway inflation. Nearly everyone will suffer.

The far right's agenda has long sought to cut taxes and use resulting deficits to restrain federal spending. Since the far right now has the balance of power in all three branches of government, the President could have controlled the purse strings without going to extreme measures. In April 2005, Federal Reserve Chairman Greenspan testified before Congress that federal budgets are on an "unsustainable path." The Chief Economist of Standard & Poors interpreted the Chairman's repeated warning as: "Why don't you idiots get this?"[10]

Much of our debt is owned by Asian countries and our own Social Security fund. However, interest in further investment may decline because of the weak dollar. For example, South Korea, the fourth largest holder of U.S. debt, said it planned to diversify into non-dollar assets—after years of holding too many low-yielding and depreciating U.S. dollar government securities.[11] What would happen if larger investors, like China, suddenly call in our debt?

As our debt increases, now 7.6 trillion, so does the annual interest we pay—$209 billion according to this year's budget. Each year, this huge expenditure absorbs a large part of the federal budget, preventing us from meeting some of our nation's most pressing needs. The amount of interest on our debt is rising every year, and it's only a matter of time before our statutory debt limit is exceeded once again.

Osama bin Laden, as an Islamic guerrilla fighter during the 1980's Afghanistan war against the Soviet Union, takes credit for having bled *that* country into bankruptcy. Now, he is taunting the U.S. over the size of our budget deficits.

A *New York Times* editorial concluded "Congress can avert

this crisis by forcing the President to be serious about deficit reduction. The first-term tax cuts should be allowed to lapse. Cuts that are not in effect should not be allowed to begin."[12]

Our country must return to fiscal sanity. It is clear that the President and his far-right advisors should face up to some tough decisions and enforce budget discipline.

Energy Independence

U.S. dependence on foreign energy sources puts us in an untenable position. For many years our foreign policy has been enslaved by our dependence on Mideast oil, and the Bush administration has made no attempt to break that stranglehold. They could have made strides toward energy independence by strongly promoting fuel-efficient products and conservation, by developing renewable and alternative energies and by raising taxes on gasoline. A major increase in gasoline taxes would help reduce both federal and trade deficits and force the auto industry to redesign their vehicles.

With U.S. oil consumption in 2001 at an all-time high, the U.S. Council on Foreign Relations warned the President that "As the 21st century opens, the energy sector is in a critical condition. A crisis could erupt at any time."[13] The President has tried several ways to increase oil supply—legislation, drilling in

Alaska, and a war in Iraq. These all failed to materialize during his first term, and gasoline prices continue to soar. In the case of Iraq, oil production is still below prewar levels and may remain so due to the insurgency.

Early in the first term the Administration was quick to submit legislation containing corporate giveaways and tax breaks for big oil, gas, and coal. That bill would perpetuate the U.S. reliance on foreign oil. It proved too expensive even for a Republican Congress to act on. Nevertheless, it has been reintroduced during the second term.[14] At a very minimum, the focus of this kind of legislation should be on helping industry develop a new generation of vehicles and substitutes for gasoline.

Instead of attempting to conserve energy, proposed legislation will allow vastly accelerated depreciation for business use of some 56 gas-guzzling SUVs. As one analyst of the legislation wrote, "Tax savings for guzzler buyers reduce government revenues, increase the federal deficit, increase our trade deficit, and send yet more money to the Middle East."[15]

The good news is that the President's 2006 budget proposal would fund hydrogen science and technologies for use in fuel-cell vehicles and electricity generation. However, experimentation with wind and solar power, and additional ways to fuel cars, were conspicuously missing. Then, when gas prices rose dramatically, Bush finally proposed an energy program.

The question is, will a comprehensive program really emerge from Congress, or is the President's rhetoric driven by politics and the need to reverse public discontent over high gas prices?

Both China and India, growing by leaps and bounds, are seriously competing with the United States to secure oil exploration rights. China is expected to have more cars than the United States in a couple of decades. The surge in demand from China and India alone may eventually outstrip supply, causing fuel prices to shoot up further. There is fear that "China and India, two energy-hungry giants seeking access to limited world resources, will inevitably clash with the West."[16]

Our health, our economy, and our environment will all be better off with a transition to renewable energy, fuel-efficient cars, and a substitute for gasoline. What we need over the long term is a truly national effort, organized by a perceptive President.

Environment

Our environment depends, to a great extent, on U.S. energy policy. Unwilling to alter that policy, the Bush administration immediately walked away from a worldwide treaty to cope with climate change and pollution. This problem is so serious that it could disrupt all civilization as we know it.[17]

The State of the Union speech offers no change in this direction. The President's budget does include some funds for various cleanup efforts, for climate-change sciences, and to spur use of energy-efficient technologies and clean, renewable energy. Progress, however, under the worldwide treaty for climate change, will be limited since the U.S. emits more greenhouse gases, like carbon dioxide, than any other nation. Our withdrawal from this treaty will hamper vital efforts to save the world from environmental dangers that are already impacting the earth's most sensitive regions.[18] Rebuffing Bush, 163 mayors in 37 states have already pledged to honor the environmental treaty.

Britain's chief scientific advisor describes global warming as a greater threat than terrorism, and Prime Minister Blair claims it is the greatest threat facing civilization. His senior scientists talk about the prospects of our world being overcome by melting ice caps, flooded cities, scorched fields, and diverted ocean currents.[19] Even our own Environmental Protection Agency's website and a secret Pentagon report warn of the dangers of rising global temperatures.

Some skeptics doubt that our planet is in grave danger from climate change, but they are vastly outnumbered by scientists. Lobbyists, funded by the U.S. oil industry, deny that these scientists are correct. One writer complained that this "is reminiscent of the tobacco lobby's attempts to persuade us smoking does not cause cancer." Some environmental changes are irreversible, such as climate change and loss of wilderness. Controlling these changes must be a priority in *every* administration.

For an excellent analysis of our environmental program today, see "For the Sake of Our Children," by Robert F. Kennedy, Jr. in the winter 2005 issue of *Earthlight*. He shows how the public is deceived by the way the Bush administration describes its environmental changes. "They want to destroy the forest, they call it the Healthy Forest Act, they want to destroy the air, they call it the Clear Skies Act."

Kennedy attributes over 400 recent major environmental rollbacks to the far right and says George W. Bush is "the worst environmental president that we have ever had." He says that, under the Bush administration, executives and lobbyists of companies that are polluters have been appointed to head up agency activities that regulate and oversee our environment. Among those cited in his article are: (1) the head of Superfund (legislative program designed to rid the country of hazardous waste sites) whose former job was to advise companies on how to evade this program, (2) the head of the EPA's Air Division who was a Monsanto lobbyist, and (3) the head of public lands who was a mining industry lobbyist and believes public lands are unconstitutional.[20]

As a general practice, industry lobbies approach Congress with pieces of legislation, contribute heavily to a congressman's campaign, and then leave with laws that favor their interests. To illustrate, let's look at how industry uses the legislative process to limit their liability on damage done to the environment.

There is a little-known provision in the President's energy bill that permits a waiver for cleanup lawsuits. These cleanups affect thousands of communities and are for smelly gasoline additives that seep into wells and foul the water. The lawsuits claim the manufacturers knew the additive would contaminate drinking water before it was widely used. In addition to the liability shield, the legislation calls for $1.75 billion in transition assistance to industry. This means taxpayers will be paying for industry cleanups. The manufacturers have contributed large sums of campaign money to House Majority Leader Tom DeLay, and this waiver is one of his top priorities.[21]

A March 2005 report, backed up by 1,360 scientists from 95 countries, some world leaders in their fields, warned that almost two-thirds of our natural machinery that supports life on earth is being degraded. "The wetlands, forest, savannahs, estuaries, coastal fisheries, and other habitants that recycle air, water and nutrients for all living creatures are being irretrievably damaged." Most of the glaciers in the Antarctic are shrinking and this retreat has accelerated. Scientists say we are living on borrowed time and depleting assets at the expense of our children.[22]

Healthcare

The President's 2006 budget proposes tax credits for low income people to purchase health insurance, tax rebates for small businesses, and partial funding of health centers serving people below the Federal Poverty Level. However, tax credits are not much benefit to low income people, and the President is cutting Medicaid, the safety net of healthcare programs, which benefits people with low incomes. This program insures 50 million children, pregnant women, elderly, and people with disabilities—our most vulnerable people.

According to the Census Bureau, there are 45 million in this country without healthcare—5 million more than when Bush first came to office. A survey, by the non-profit Robert Wood Foundation, shows that 20 of the 45 million are people with jobs but without health insurance. 41% of these have trouble seeing a doctor when they need to and 56% do not have a personal doctor. Even those with health insurance have problems. Many have inferior insurance and can be ruined by illness and medical bills they can't pay. In addition, illness can lead to job loss, and job loss can lead to loss of insurance.[23]

Most industrialized nations have a comprehensive health program for their citizens. There is no reason we, the world's largest and wealthiest nation, should not see to it that every working American has access to basic and affordable healthcare. In

March 2005, the American Progress Action Fund proposed a plan, building on the strengths of our current system, and a conglomerate industry group is working on another plan.[24]

By restricting government funding for stem cell research, the President has severely hampered progress toward finding cures for chronic diseases that cripple, and sometimes kill, thousands of Americans. He made a token gesture by authorizing research on a handful of already existing stem cell lines but, according to research scientists, most of those lines are contaminated or corrupted and are unusable.

The Congress favors federal funding for research using those embryos that are already being discarded, as unneeded surplus, by in vitro fertilization clinics all over this country. A House bill requires informed consent of the donor couples, bans any buying or selling of embryos, and includes clear ethical guidelines for the research. It has more than 200 co-sponsors from both sides of the aisle. President Bush has not vetoed a single bill in over 4 years in office, but he's threatening a veto on this one.

The far right argues that research using embryos is destroying human life. Actually, donating embryos that are going to be discarded anyway would be very similar to organ donation, which helps save countless lives each year. Why not use something that would otherwise be thrown away to help alleviate the pain and suffering of many?

The U.S. was a leader in stem cell research, but with limited government support here, we are falling far behind other countries that have the full support of their governments. This will soon precipitate a brain drain of our top scientists in the field. There is simply not enough private funding for their research to make real progress here.

California has started a new $3 billion state-financed stem cell research institute. High-profile Republicans, like Governor Schwarzenegger, Nancy Reagan, and Senator John McCain are outspoken in their support for stem cell research.

Watching potential life-saving research making progress in other countries, and realizing that our government is trying to slow down or halt such research here, is very frustrating for the handicapped. President Bush campaigned in 2000 as a "Compassionate Conservative," but where's the compassion since he took office? It's certainly not evident in the healthcare field.

Social Security

For decades the far right has wanted to dismantle Franklin Roosevelt's tremendously-popular Social Security program. Now, they have conceived a way to do it.

The President declared in his State of the Union speech that the system is going bankrupt but offered no specific plan to fix it. He overstated the crisis, and many believe Social Security is

sustainable with minor modifications such as raising the retirement age or the $90,000 salary cap on Social Security taxes.[25]
At the same time, the President proposed something that would
worsen the so-called financial "crisis." His proposal would
divert monies away from the Social Security trust fund to private accounts, with a transition cost of nearly $5 trillion over
several decades.[26] The U.S. is already overburdened with
huge budget deficits and would have to borrow more money to
finance this approach. As one writer said, that's money "we
don't have, can't afford, and would have to borrow with hor-
rid economic consequences."

The basic problem is that the President advertises his plan
as a way to fix Social Security when, in reality, it would grad-
ually destroy the program. The system is certainly not going
bankrupt—$150 billion in Social Security surplus for this year
is financing government spending and the President's tax cuts.

The President proposed that part of an individual's Social
Security deductions that would normally go into the Social
Security trust fund be invested in a private or personal account.
Many invest their *own* money today in 401Ks and IRAs, but that
supplements, rather than replaces, Social Security. Under
Bush's plan we would invest money the government has *loaned*
us and pay interest to the government on that loan. An individual would eventually get any return on his investment *that
exceeds the interest*.[27] Otherwise, he ends up with less than is

offered by the current system.

There also will be benefit cuts to middle and higher income people, and retirees will be required to use part of their personal accounts to buy an annuity. The benefit cuts would be substantial to middle income people but hardly felt by the wealthy. Critics argue that this approach would convert a retirement system to a poverty program.

Basically, Social Security is an insurance program, not an investment or poverty program. If the new investor stays with safe stocks and bonds, he will not do much better than he would in the current system. If he risks more, there goes the "safety net"—guaranteed income that a lot of retirees depend on. Other problems include a possible financial catastrophe for those who invest unwisely or are victims of market conditions when they retire—a bust instead of a boom. And, what happens to workers who opt out of the traditional system and then become disabled? Now, they draw disability payments from Social Security and can pass them on to their widow and underage children after they die. There is nothing in the President's proposal that addresses this problem.

Twice, the President has misused the highly-regarded Senator Moynihan to support his reform of Social Security—once in a debate with Senator Kerry and again during his State of the Union speech. Since, sadly, the Senator is no longer around to defend himself, his daughter, Maura Moynihan, wrote an article correcting the record. She made clear that her father proposed individual accounts simply as "add-ons" that would supplement Social Security. Senator Moynihan went to great lengths in the 1980's to save Social Security and extend the system until 2060. Her father, she said, "was committed to honoring the contract the government made with its citizens," and he believed the far right was determined to undermine that contract.[28]

Private accounts have encountered a variety of problems in other countries.[29]

Education

In a global economy, education represents the long-term future of our country. Some past presidents have called themselves "The Education President." None have earned that label, and our students have fallen behind those of many other countries.

Early in his first term the President created a program called "No Child Left Behind." But, the program certainly hasn't lived up to its name. The President and Congress haven't made it a priority and have failed to fully fund it. Several states are either challenging the law or are suing to free themselves from requirements not funded by the federal government. A frequent criticism of the law is that one set of rules doesn't fit all students.

A year-long bipartisan study by the National Conference of State Legislatures concluded that the program is flawed. Among other things, it has undermined school improvement efforts, relied on the wrong indicators, usurped state and local control of public schools, and failed to recognize educational challenges by teachers across the nation. According to the study, the program is excessively intrusive in the day-to-day operations of public education.[30]

The President's 2006 education budget would increase the funding for "No Child Left Behind" and extend that program to high schools. The new budget proposes funds to help needy students and to attract and train high-quality teachers. But, if you take a closer look at the budget, you'll find a $9 billion dollar shortfall to fund school reforms. Head Start, child care, literacy programs, after-school programs, as well as support for vocational education have been cut, while college costs are becoming increasingly unreachable by many working families. Trailers are already overused as classrooms, but monies for school construction and maintenance have also been cut.[31]

The President's priorities are misplaced. His legacy and our country would be vastly improved if he spent more time insuring that our youth receive a first-class education and less time pushing an ill-conceived war and radical Social Security reform.

Religion

Our founding fathers were intent on keeping church and state firmly separated. This constitutional separation has been eroded by the Bush administration. The President relies on his "gut" or his "instinct," rather than on facts and advice in making important decisions. One high official from the first Bush administration said, "He truly believes he's on a mission from God." Some of his followers are even convinced that he is "a divinely chosen instrument of God."[32]

America was created to permit freedom of worship of *any* religion, an essential guarantee. An author on this subject has raised the question: are we a "society of inclusion, reason, diversity, and individual faith, or are we mandated to be a certain kind of intolerant Christian society?"[33] According to Walter Cronkite, the religious right is, "...manipulating religion to further their intolerant, political agenda."

In particular, the President has used the very personal and private matter of religion to convey to the public that he consulted God on his decision to go to war. But, would God have condoned war, when it was *not* the last resort? Would God have risked exposing hundreds of thousands of soldiers, innocent civilians and children to death, permanent disability and long-term mental disorders? And, as the war drags on, are we all becoming increasingly indifferent to the suffering and loss of life that only affects others?

Is the Bush administration politicizing religion, and are they being hypocritical? Contrary to the teachings of most religions, their actions have favored, from the very beginning, the well-off, not the poor, weak, and downtrodden. Episcopal minister and former Republican U.S. Senator, John Danforth, claims his party's fixation on a religious agenda has turned them in the wrong direction. It is time, he says, for Republicans to rediscover their roots and worry about rising deficits.[34]

Any president's spiritual life is personal, and his work must stand or fall on its own merit. He should not suggest to the public that he knows God's will. President Lincoln had it right—*don't try to prove God is on your side, prove that you are on God's side.*

Anyone with an interest in this subject must read, and discuss with others, an article, by Rev. Dr. Graham Standish "Forum: A Country Divided by Christ." (Appendix II).

Abuses of Power Early in Second Term

In addition to governing improperly, the far right continues to abuse power into the second Bush term.

The far right has a plan, referred to as the "nuclear option," to change congressional rules and eliminate filibusters. Filibusters are the only tool the minority can use to challenge reckless behavior. If enacted, the "nuclear option" would eliminate checks and balances, a vital part of our democracy for over 200 years. Basically, this is a far-right bid for absolute power.

Congress and the President recently stripped Florida of its

jurisdiction, trying to overrule state courts and nearly 20 judges on a right-to-life issue that had been litigated many times over the years. A Republican jurist, who is one of the most conservative on the Federal bench, ruled against this Federal interference, upholding the state courts. He said the congressional/presidential action was "demonstrably at odds with our Founding Fathers' blueprint for governance of a free people—our Constitution."

The far-right leadership in the House of Representatives made extraordinary changes to the Ethics Committee to shield Tom DeLay from further congressional investigation (p. 53). They replaced the Republican Chairman and two moderate Republicans with DeLay allies. They also changed the rules so that, acting alone, the new Republican membership could block an investigation. Democrats refused to go along with this sham, effectively shutting down the Ethics Committee. The House leadership finally reversed its Ethics Committee rule changes. However, the committee is stalled again because of a disagreement over filling the Chief of Staff position. A *New York Times* article summarizes the situation:

"DeLay's ethical and financial lapses are serious and disqualifying for his high office. But even more alarming than his love for political money is his abuse of power....DeLay is not content with having a Republican president and majorities in both houses of Congress. He wants to control every aspect of government fully....The method is simple. When the game does not go his way, he changes the rules. If Republicans cannot win huge majorities in House races, he shifts the boundaries of their districts; if ethics rules start to catch up with his reckless behavior, he rewrites them."[35]

The Bottom Line

Far-right extreme politics have led the Republican Party out of the American mainstream. As pointed out in a *St. Louis Post-Dispatch* commentary of March 2005, the President's friendly personality and real-guy persona have blurred the true nature of his radical agenda. This agenda has included a go-it-alone foreign policy, a unilateral war policy, running up huge deficits, making the U.S. more, rather than less, dependent on Mideast oil, overriding decades of environmental protection, and "junking" Social Security.

As one analyst describes the situation, the Bush Administration creates an illusion of how the world works, and then makes policy based on that illusion. What makes the situation dangerous is that the Administration really believes its illusion is the reality.

A poll conducted in 2005, shows that in an imaginary contest between the moderate Bill Clinton and the far-right George Bush, Clinton beat Bush 53 percent to 43 percent. As one columnist said, this is a decisive judgment on the two most recent political legacies.

What this nation sorely needs is new moderate leadership, from either political party—leadership that will unite the country and get us back on track with some well-thought-out, long-term solutions to our *real* problems. The mission would be to focus on our most pressing ones and make the kind of progress that succeeding presidents can build on. Wild swings, due to the far right's misuse of power, must end.

Americans can no longer afford to be apathetic and uninformed—and susceptible to the Administration's propaganda and deception. It's time to put our democracy back to work.

"Let us stand back in awe at the Bush administration's genius. Few administrations in our history have been more successful in setting the terms of the political debate. None has been as skilled at getting its facts accepted as plausible even when they are not. None has looked so principled, even when it said one thing while doing another."

—E. J. Dionne, *Washington Post*, February 11, 2005

Endnotes

1 "Bush silence would speak to Europe" Tom Friedman, *New York Times,* February 1, 2005.

2 "Wars put U.S. forces at risk abroad, Myers says" *Los Angeles Times*, May 3, 2005.

3 "The coalition of the wilting" *Chicago Tribune*, March 21, 2005; "Body Counts" Christopher Dickey, *Newsweek*, May 13, 2003.

4 "U. S. missile defense fails again" *New York Times*, February 15, 2005; "Rumsfeld makes case for funding missile defense" Tom Squitieri, *USA Today*, February18, 2005.

5 "The Real Missile Defense Gap" David Ignatius, *Washington Post*, March 23, 2005.

6 "Apocalypse Soon" Robert S. McNamara, *Foreign Policy*, May/June 2005.

7 "Bush silence would speak to Europe" Tom Friedman, *New York Times*, February 1, 2005; "America, a Symbol of..." Bob Herbert, *New York Times*, May 30, 2005.

8 "Why can't (won't) Georgie add?" Jac Wilder VerSterg, *Palm Beach Post*, February 14, 2005.

9 "After Bush Leaves Office, His Budget's Costs Balloon" *Washington Post*, February 15, 2005; "H. Ross Perot, the U.S. Needs You" Tom Blackburn, *Palm Beach Post*, March 14, 2005.

10 "Second thoughts, Fed chief acknowledges 2001 tax cuts encouraged deficit" Neil Henderson, *Washington Post*, April 22, 2005; "Attention: Deficit Disorder" Robert Rubin, *New York Times*, May 13, 2005.

11 "Dollar shrinks awash in bad policy" Tom Friedman, *New York Times*, February 2005.

12 "The Importance of Being Earnest" *New York Times*, February 14, 2005.

13 "U.S. appears to have fought the war for oil and lost it" Ian Rutledge, *FT.com*, April 11, 2005; "Energy Insanity" Molly Ivins, *Working For Change*, March 29, 2005.

14 "The Missing Energy Strategy" *New York Times* editorial, April 19, 2005.

15 "Guzzle away—Uncle Sam's buying" Scott Burns, *Universal Press Syndicate*, April 18, 2005; "No Mullah Left Behind" Tom Friedman, *New York Times*, February 13, 2005.

16 "The Axis of Oil" *In These Times*, February 2, 2005.

17 "A Climate of Disdain" *Washington Post*, February 9, 2005; "A Warming Climate" *Washington Post*, January 28, 2005.

18 "Kyoto pact begins with eye toward U.S." *Associated Press*, February 17, 2005.

19 "How we put the heat on nature" *Guardian Unlimited*, January 30, 2005.

20 "Kennedy Bashes Bush for Crime against Nature" *Common Dreams News Center,* Jan. 25, 2005; "For the Sake of Our Children" Robert Kennedy, Jr., *EarthLight*, Winter 2005

21 "A Dirty Little Footnote to the Energy Bill" Alexei Barrionnuevo, *New York Times*, April 15, 2005; "Embattled DeLay At Center Of Fight To Protect MTBE Makers" *Associated Press*, April 12, 2005.

22 "Two-thirds of world resources used up" Tim Radford, Science Editor, *Guardian Unlimited*, March 30, 2005.

23 "Study: 20 million U.S. Workers Lack Health Insurance" *Reuters*, April 27, 2005; "No insurance against going broke" *Washington Post*, February 2005.

24 "A Principled and Practical Plan to Provide Health Care for All Americans" *American Progress Action Fund*, March 23, 2005;

"An Urgent Case For Fixing Health Care" David Broder, *Washington Post*, May 29, 2005.

25 "Privatization: No brains, no security" *Palm Beach Post*, February 14, 2005.

26 "Read The Fine Print" *New York Times*, Feb. 6, 2005; "Haste Makes Waste" David Broder, *Washington Post*, May 5, 2005.

27 "Participants Would Forfeit Part of Account's Profits" *Washington Post*, February 3, 2005; "They Invested Years in Private Accounts" *Los Angeles Times*, January 31, 2005; "The Risks in Personal Accounts" *Washington Post* Editorial, February 20, 2005.

28 "Don't take his name in vain," Maura Moynihan, *Daily News*, February 27, 2005.

29 "Social Security reform a bumpy ride" Matt Moffett, *Wall Street Journal,* February 6, 2005; "A Personal Burden" Marie Dickerson, *Los Angeles Times*, Feb. 13, 2005; "Gambling with your Retirement" Paul Krugman, *New York Times*, February 4, 2005.

30 "Report: 'No Child' Law Amiss" *New York Times*, Feb. 24, 2005; "Lawsuit Targets No Child Left Behind" *New York Times*, April 21, 2005.

31 "Squandering America's Future" Robert Borosage, *Tom Paine*

Common Sense, February 8, 2005.

32 "What makes Bush's presidency so radical" Ron Suskind, *New York Times Magazine*, October 17, 2004; "Ex-Aide Questions Bush Vow to Back Faith-Based Efforts" Alan Cooperman and Jim Vanderhel, *Washington Post,* February 15, 2005.

33 Jacoby, Susan, *Freethinkers: A History of American Secularism*, Owl Books, 2nd Reprint Edition, January 7, 2005.

34 "In the Name of Politics" John Danforth, *New York Times*, March 30, 2005.

35 "Tom DeLay's Power Trip" *New York Times*, April 18, 2005.

Appendix I

U.S. Diplomat's Letter of Resignation

(as printed on *nytimes.com;* Rep. Hon. Fortney Pete Stark of California read this
letter into the *Congressional Record* (Extensions) (Page E363-E364)
on March 4, 2003.)

*The following is the text of John Brady Kiesling's letter of resignation to
Secretary of State Colin L. Powell. Mr. Kiesling is a career diplomat who has
served in United States embassies from Tel Aviv to Casablanca to Yerevan.*

Dear Mr. Secretary:

I am writing you to submit my resignation from the Foreign Service
of the United States and from my position as Political Counselor in U.S.
Embassy Athens, effective March 7. I do so with a heavy heart. The bag-
gage of my upbringing included a felt obligation to give something back
to my country. Service as a U.S. diplomat was a dream job. I was paid to
understand foreign languages and cultures, to seek out diplomats, politicians, scholars and journalists, and to persuade them that U.S. interests
and theirs fundamentally coincided. My faith in my country and its values
was the most powerful weapon in my diplomatic arsenal.

It is inevitable that during twenty years with the State Department I
would become more sophisticated and cynical about the narrow and selfish
bureaucratic motives that sometimes shaped our policies. Human nature is
what it is, and I was rewarded and promoted for understanding human
nature. But until this Administration it had been possible to believe that by
upholding the policies of my president I was also upholding the interests of
the American people and the world. I believe it no longer.

The policies we are now asked to advance are incompatible not only
with American values but also with American interests. Our fervent pursuit

of war with Iraq is driving us to squander the international legitimacy that has been America's most potent weapon of both offense and defense since the days of Woodrow Wilson. We have begun to dismantle the largest and most effective web of international relationships the world has ever known. Our current course will bring instability and danger, not security.

The sacrifice of global interests to domestic politics and to bureaucratic self-interest is nothing new, and it is certainly not a uniquely American problem. Still, we have not seen such systematic distortion of intelligence, such systematic manipulation of American opinion, since the war in Vietnam. The September 11 tragedy left us stronger than before, rallying around us a vast international coalition to cooperate for the first time in a systematic way against the threat of terrorism. But rather than take credit for those successes and build on them, this Administration has chosen to make terrorism a domestic political tool, enlisting a scattered and largely defeated Al Qaeda as its bureaucratic ally. We spread disproportionate terror and confusion in the public mind, arbitrarily linking the unrelated problems of terrorism and Iraq. The result, and perhaps the motive, is to justify a vast misallocation of shrinking public wealth to the military and to weaken the safeguards that protect American citizens from the heavy hand of government. September 11 did not do as much damage to the fabric of American society as we seem determined to [do] to ourselves. Is the Russia of the late Romanovs really our model, a selfish, superstitious empire thrashing toward self-destruction in the name of a doomed status quo?

We should ask ourselves why we have failed to persuade more of the world that a war with Iraq is necessary. We have over the past two years done too much to assert to our world partners that narrow and mercenary U.S. interests override the cherished values of our partners. Even where our aims were not in question, our consistency is at issue. The model of Afghanistan is little comfort to allies wondering on what basis we plan to rebuild the Middle East, and in whose image and interests. Have we indeed become blind, as Russia is blind in Chechnya, as Israel is blind in the Occupied Territories, to our own advice, that overwhelming military power is not the answer to terrorism? After the shambles of post-war Iraq joins the shambles in Grozny and Ramallah, it will be a brave foreigner who forms ranks with Micronesia to follow where we lead.

We have a coalition still, a good one. The loyalty of many of our friends is impressive, a tribute to American moral capital built up over a century. But our closest allies are persuaded less that war is justified than that it would be perilous to allow the U.S. to drift into complete solipsism. Loyalty should be reciprocal. Why does our President condone the swaggering and contemptuous approach to our friends and allies this Administration is fostering, including among its most senior officials. Has "oderint dum metuant" really become our motto?

I urge you to listen to America's friends around the world. Even here in Greece, purported hotbed of European anti-Americanism, we have more and closer friends than the American newspaper reader can possibly imagine. Even when they complain about American arrogance, Greeks know that the world is a difficult and dangerous place, and they want a strong international system, with the U.S. and EU in close partnership. When our friends are afraid of us rather than for us, it is time to worry. And now they are afraid. Who will tell them convincingly that the United States is as it was, a beacon of liberty, security, and justice for the planet?

Mr. Secretary, I have enormous respect for your character and ability. You have preserved more international credibility for us than our policy deserves, and salvaged something positive from the excesses of an ideological and self-serving Administration. But your loyalty to the President goes too far. We are straining beyond its limits an international system we built with such toil and treasure, a web of laws, treaties, organizations, and shared values that sets limits on our foes far more effectively than it ever constrained America's ability to defend its interests.

I am resigning because I have tried and failed to reconcile my conscience with my ability to represent the current U.S. Administration. I have confidence that our democratic process is ultimately self-correcting, and hope that in a small way I can contribute from outside to shaping policies that better serve the security and prosperity of the American people and the world we share.

Appendix II

Article by Rev. Dr. Graham Standish published on *Post-gazette.com*
June 12, 2005

Forum: A Country Divided by Christ

If you are a Christian, how should you vote, Republican or Democrat? As a seminary student in the 1980s, the choice seemed clear, at least for many of my classmates. We could not be Christian and Republican. We especially could not be Christian and vote for Ronald Reagan. The only choice was to be a Democrat. You can imagine that I felt a bit odd being a registered Republican who happened to vote for Ronald Reagan...twice. Apparently I wasn't much of a Christian back then.

How time changes everything. Today, Christians all over the country, in print and on conservative talk radio, suggest that the only political option for Christians is to be Republican. During the last election, churches nationwide urged their members, and Christians their friends, to vote for George W. Bush. They simultaneously attacked John Kerry's faith, suggesting that he should be barred from Roman Catholic communion because of his political beliefs. Apparently, to be a Christian now means to be a Republican.

Ironically, I left the Republican Party in 1992 and registered as an independent precisely because I sensed the Republican Party slipping away from the Christianity to which I had committed my life. Why? Among other things, I could no longer abide the Republican-sanctioned, Lee Atwater-orchestrated style of politics in which politicians attack, denigrate, eviscerate and even falsely accuse each other. This was a style of politics that became a mainstay of the 1988 elections and remains a staple of politics today. It skirts the issues in favor of assailing the character of the enemy.

This attack-and-accuse style of politics has grown fiercer over the years, yet it conflicts with a Christian Gospel that says "love your enemies, bless those who curse you, do good to those who hate you and pray for those who persecute you," and to "be completely humble and gentle; be patient, bearing one another in love."

For a time I considered joining the Democratic Party, but they seemed to have little interest in people of faith, and my leanings are still more Republican than Democrat. I still share many of the Republican economic and social beliefs, but I'm left in a quandary, and I'm not alone.

There are millions of Christians who lean Republican, but have found that the Christianity of the Republican Party is a strand of Christianity that promotes a narrow Gospel, while ignoring much of what Christianity has always taught about caring for the poor, the virtues of sacrificing self for the welfare of others, and the need for humility, compassion and peace.

Too many Republican Party leaders have aligned themselves with a fundamentalist brand of Protestant Christianity characterized by black-and-white, us-versus-them perspectives: we're saved, you're not; we're right, you're wrong; we conservatives are right and virtuous, you liberals are wrong and sinful.

This kind of thinking bleeds into their political rhetoric as they assert a kind of divine mandate for proposed programs and platforms. The Republican Party has been guided in this way of politicking by fundamentalists like Jerry Falwell, Pat Robertson, Ralph Reed, Rick Scarborough of the Patriot Pastors Network and James Dobson of Focus on the Family, among others, who have an agenda to make the United States a so-called "Christian" nation, with little room for Christians like me with different perspectives. Many of them call themselves evangelicals, despite the fact that the evangelical viewpoint actually is much broader and allows for much more diversity of opinion and belief.

188

Fundamentalism isn't restricted to American politics. Religious fundamentalism has a grip on much of the world. We are in an international struggle against fundamentalist Muslim terrorists who want to create truly "Muslim" nations to counteract a modern world that has strayed too far from the Quran. Israel struggles to appease Jewish fundamentalists who believe that abandoning settlements in the West Bank erodes Israel's divine rights as a "Jewish" nation. Even the Roman Catholic Church is grappling with its own fundamentalists who want to return the church to its pre-Vatican II days.

Why do so many non-fundamentalist Christians follow fundamentalist agendas, especially when it comes to politics? One answer is that influential fundamentalists have learned to articulate rigid beliefs in a moderate and compelling language that softens the hardness of their position.

For example, in Kansas, fundamentalists have put their weight behind a proposal that "intelligent design" be taught in biology classes. Intelligent design is an idea that sounds very much like what the Roman Catholic Church and most mainline Protestant churches worldwide believe: that while evolution may be the mechanism of creation, God is the architect, engineer and project manager. Fundamentalists hope that the teaching of "intelligent design" in schools will take them one step closer to barring the teaching of evolution in schools. What they don't reveal is their belief that there is only one truth: their religious truth. There is little room for thinking that integrates the insights of both religion and science.

Fundamentalists have also learned to employ an issue-reduction strategy using people and their stories to oversimplify complex issues in order to promote a fundamentalist ideology.

The Terry Schiavo case was a great example of this. Fundamentalists who heavily influence the Republican Party used her to reframe the issue of euthanasia by reducing it to a portrayal of a virtuous family trying to keep a disabled (they refused to call her comatose) woman alive, while her evil husband tried to kill her. They prompted the media and Republican rhetoric with all sorts of unsubstantiated accusations that Michael Schiavo was a greedy and abusive husband who wanted to kill Terry for his own personal gain. In doing so, they reduced the larger issue of euthanasia to a simple equation they hoped all would agree with: extending life is virtuous, while euthanasia is evil.

What they didn't expect was that the majority of Americans, especially mainstream Christians, many of whom have grappled with end-of-life issues in their own families, believe that this issue is not so simple. They also never proposed an alternative Christian suggestion, one that is very much in keeping with the biblical mandate to make "every effort to maintain the unity of the Spirit in the bond of peace." What would have happened if Christians had encouraged this traumatized and divided family to seek reconciliation and to prayerfully discern an answer together? What if Republican politicians had united all of us behind this kind of solution rather than reducing the issue to a divisive one of good versus evil?

This current mixture of Christianity and politics is troublesome because the more religion identifies with a particular political movement, the more that movement erodes religion. Politics, by its very nature, is a realm that is often tainted by pride and a desire for power that can bring out the worst in humans because the pursuit of power corrupts. It's for this reason that Jesus said we should render unto Caesar that which is Ceasar's, and render unto God that which is God's. Mixing politics and religion causes too many people to confuse Caesar's empire with God's kingdom.

Religion does have a place in political discourse, yet Christians need to be sure they don't confuse a politically expedient position with God's position. God's position is often unclear, especially in many of the gray areas of life. Presenting one political party as "the Christian party" is particularly troublesome because distilling religious faith down to political terms drains religion of its ability to lead people to move beyond a politics of self-interest.

Misuse of Power

Party affiliation doesn't make a person a Christian. There are millions of Christians who serve Christ faithfully as members of both major political parties; for each party represents particular concerns of Christianity, but neither captures them entirely. The Republicans are not the Christian party, even if millions of Christians are Republicans.

I believe that those of us who are Christian and take politics seriously need to resist the tendency to align our beliefs to strongly with any particular political movement.

Christians need to find a way to take the Gospel seriously, while simultaneously avoiding the assumption that one political party can embody the concerns of our faith. And if we are true to our faith, we need to embrace a political stance that expects politicians to seek solutions in line with our beliefs, and in a way that seeks unity rather than division.

Perhaps it is time to expect more from Republican and Democratic politicians, demanding that if they proclaim a Christian mantle, they begin acting with Christian regard for others, even their enemies, even each other.

Acknowledgements

As other authors have recognized, any book is the collective work of untold people who have contributed ideas, knowledge, insights, and recollections. We owe an immense debt to those who have researched and written extensively about the impeachment saga, 9/11, the war in Iraq, and the President's national defense and domestic programs.

We owe a very special thanks to our patient and perceptive chief editor, Lynn Hall, for her continuing assistance on this book. She improved each of the many drafts and sometimes sent back tough questions for us to grapple with.

We very much appreciate the enthusiasm and willingness of Mayhaven Publishing to back this book and put it on a fast track.

There are two other publishers who showed support for this project. Ward Morehouse, President and Publisher of Apex Press took a personal interest from the very beginning. His feedback included the idea that sparked the last chapter—one that takes the reader into the President's second term. Chaz Bufe of See Sharp Press simply did not have the resources to commit to this book but volunteered to recommend it to other publishers. His encouragement, advice, and high professional standards meant a lot to us.

Our Republican friend, responsible for the two quotes at the beginning of the book, is Jill Melmed Buzzeo, formerly co-founder and executive of an investment firm. She wrote these words as part of a letter to a Republican friend just before the 2004 election. She has a deep and abiding interest in the future welfare of our country.

We gained additional insight into far-right excesses from material on the *Buzzflash* and *MoveOn.org* websites. We also received valuable feedback on our manuscript from a close friend, Dr. Charles Stenger, and family members Julian and Mickey Hall.

Finally, we and the entire country owe a large debt of gratitude to the 9/11 families, whose amazing persistence overcame the President's opposition to an independent investigation of the 9/11 disaster.